Marching as to War

Personal Narratives of African American Women's Experiences in the Gulf Wars

Elizabeth F. Desnoyers-Colas

University Press of America,® Inc.
Lanham • Boulder • New York • Toronto • Plymouth, UK

This book is especially dedicated to:

My parents Josephus and Carolyn,
who helped me begin this military life journey

My siblings Peter and Lucinda,
who joined me on this military life journey

James and Sharon Neel,
who helped sustain me on this military life journey

Rosa Lee Watts, Carrie Harris, Judith Robinson—
great educators who taught me the importance of loving reading, music,
languages and science early on in this military life journey

Dr. Michael P. Graves, a master rhetorician
who taught me the importance of crafting meaningful narratives and
bringing them to literary life.

Shoshana Johnson, a noble and courageous soul
whose Operation Iraqi Freedom Prisoner of War journey was and is the
quintessential saga of 21st century African American female military
service.

Contents

Acknowledgments   vii

1   Marching as to War: Personal Narratives of African American Women's Experiences in the Gulf Wars   1

2   Why We Serve: An Historical Overview of African American Women's Military Service from the Revolutionary War through the Gulf Wars   19

3   "Sistahs" of Defense: Duties and Dangers of African American Women in Service in the Gulf Wars   41

4   My Child Left Behind: The Family and Child Care Challenges Faced by African American Gulf War Servicewomen   59

5   What Happens in the Desert Stays in the Desert: African American Women Confront Racism and Sexism in the Gulf   77

6   Where My Health Comes From: African American Servicewomen Battle Gulf War Illnesses   95

Epilogue: Marching as to War—Final Thoughts   111

Bibliography   115

Index   119

Acknowledgments

Works of this magnitude take a whole literary support village to bring it to publication fruition. It is in this light that I take this opportunity to thank a few of those villagers who made this work possible:

University Press of America's Vice President and Director Julie Kirsch and Acquisitions Editor Laura Espinoza provided constant support and encouragement. Thank you for your unflagging belief in this work, your spirited defense of it when needed and your continued assistance. You have both made this a delightful, unforgettably wonderful literary experience. An American Fellowship from the American Association of University Women helped fund much needed research time. Thanks for supporting important academic work about African American women who served and continue to serve their country.

Works gleaned from Women in Military Service Memorial Oral History Archives Collections aided immeasurably in the writing of my book chapters one and two.

Paul Ingram, my hard working editor and determined wordsmith also believed in this work and treated it with dignity and respect. His suggestions for changes and clarity were always given with grace. His expertise was greatly appreciated and needed.

Dr. Tom Cato, Chair of the Armstrong Atlantic State University Arts, Music and Theater Department is a great colleague and wonderful boss. From the outset of this work he actively supported my research agenda.

Dr. Gary Edgerton, professor and dean of the College of Communication at Butler University, Dr. Richard Norquist, professor emeritus, Armstrong Atlantic State University, Dr. Pamela Corpron Parker, professor of English, Whitworth University graciously provided their long term support to this project. I thank you all for your senior colleague support of this academic endeavor.

The National Association of Black Military Women provided key historical archival information. The NABMW continued urging African American women veterans to "tell herstory" helped me keep my eyes and empirical focus on this literary prize.

I especially thank the women whose riveting narratives brought this book to life: Carolyn, Coreen, Courtney, Felecia, Gidgetti, Gwendolyn, Hearther, Jacqueline, Kim, Maria, Patricia candidly told their stories often through laughter, tears and triumph. Thank you for your military service and willingness to share your stories with the world.

Chapter One

Marching as to War

*Personal Narratives of
African American Women's Experiences
in the Gulf Wars*

Soldiery is associated with strong, brave men. That's the way it used to be before gender equality changed the definition. Rewind and come again. Today's soldiers are supposed to be strong men AND women marching off to war, with the cross of freedom going on before, right?
—Barbara Gloudon, Jamaican journalist and playwright

There has been little in history books that either includes women or focuses on them. This has been especially true for military histories, even more so for military women . . . .
—Lorry Fenner, military historian and former Air Force intelligence officer

History belongs to she who holds the pen.
—Julianne Malveaux, Ph.D., economist and social commentator

U.S. Army Specialist Shoshana Johnson sat rigidly in a chair and glanced furtively at her captors. On the video tape it appeared that she was disoriented and seemed terrified, dazed, and confused. As she responded softly and haltingly to the gruff questions phrased in heavily accented English by an off-camera Iraqi interrogator, she looked pleadingly in that person's direction, as if asking, "What do you want me to say? Why are you making me do this?"

Throughout the five-minute interview, viewed by millions worldwide, she winced as if in physical pain.

For her captors, the capture and display of Specialist Johnson provided an opportunity to bask in the global media spotlight. She provided an important propaganda moment, orchestrated to show the world the "humane" manner in which the Iraqi army treated one of its newly acquired U.S. female prisoners of war. This was an African American soldier, captured less than a week after the March 2003 launch of Operation Iraqi Freedom.

For me, watching that scene as it played out on a grainy video in a "CNN Breaking News" report forever changed my view of the historical significance and value of black women in military service to the United States.

As for Specialist Johnson, her capture was doubtless the last thing U.S. senior military and executive branch officials wanted to have publicized. Any sustained media focus on U.S. POWS, especially a female POW, could quickly derail the upbeat government campaign. The U.S. government was hyping the angle that "all is well with the war; we're still shocking and awing." Nonetheless, that videotaped confirmation of her capture was an unexpected historical moment in the making, propelling Shoshana Johnson into the annals of history as the first African American female prisoner of war in any U.S. military conflict.

At the time of her capture, Shoshana served as a cook in the U.S. Army's 507th Maintenance Company. In mid-February 2003, the eighty-two-member company left its home base at Fort Bliss, Texas, near El Paso, and arrived in Kuwait. It remained there for a month to prepare and undergo additional training for its upcoming primary support mission in Operation Iraqi Freedom—providing equipment and vehicle repair and maintenance for Central Command's patriot missile battalion (5th Battalion, 52nd Air Defense Artillery). On March 20, the 507th entered Southeastern Iraq in a large convoy, along with other Army and Marine Corps units and other coalition combat ground forces.

Quickly caught up in the war's frenetic pace, the 507th sped toward its attack support destination. The unit barely stopped, slept, or ate over the next three days. At some point, the convoy became lost and got separated from its parent unit, the 3rd Forward Support Battalion.

In a frantic effort to catch up, the 507th company commander decided to split the convoy into three smaller elements. That action proved to be a tragic mistake.

Just after dawn on March 23, as the newly divided company elements attempted to pass through one of the coalition checkpoints in An Nasiriya, each element came under attack from Iraqi forces. Two elements successfully eluded enemy advances and managed to engage the Iraqi forces in brief combat before getting through the checkpoint. The third was not so fortunate. For more than an hour, determined Iraqi forces mounted a swarming, relentless attack, eventually overwhelming the thirty-three-member unit, of which

Shoshana was a member. An official U.S. Army investigative report, released July 17, 2003, summarizes the element's fate:

> The element of the 507th Maintenance Company that bravely fought through An Nasiriya found itself in a desperate situation due to a navigational error caused by the combined effects of the operational pace, acute fatigue, isolation, and the harsh conditions. The tragic results of this error placed the soldiers of the 507th Maintenance Company in a torrent of fire from an adaptive enemy employing asymmetrical tactics. [1]

The skirmish ended with eleven U.S. soldiers killed and six taken prisoner by Iraqi irregular forces. Sixteen of the element's members evaded capture and were later rescued by U.S. Marines. Two women soldiers besides Shoshana were in the unit. Private Jessica Lynch, a White supply clerk, was severely wounded, captured, and taken to an Iraqi hospital. Private First Class Lori Ann Piestewa was also severely injured when the Humvee she was driving was hit by explosives and crashed into another Humvee. Lynch was in Piestewa's Humvee. Piestewa was taken to the same Iraqi hospital as Lynch but did not survive her injuries. She was initially classified as Missing in Action, but her body was found later, buried in an unmarked grave with the bodies of the other soldiers who had died in the ambush. U.S. forces later recovered their remains. Piestewa was the first Native American woman killed in combat and the first U.S. servicewoman to die in Operation Iraqi Freedom.

The fate of these three women substantively affected the previously unresolved issue of women's place in combat. Barely three years into the 21st century, America's military had to acknowledge and contend realistically with a gargantuan elephant of an issue that was crowding the Pentagon's battle planning room. The sheer number of deployed women had begun to force the military's hand on the issue of women in combat.

It was not always that way for servicewomen.

As the daughter of a male African American U.S. Army staff sergeant in the post-Korea-Vietnam-war era, I grew up believing that "real women" did not go to war or want to go to war. In fact, "real" women would not even go into the military unless they were looking for a husband, were not physically attractive enough to acquire a husband, or were gay and didn't need or want a husband.

As a nomadic "female Army brat," I also quickly learned that the primary purpose of a "real woman" (i.e., a female military spouse) was to care for her conquering male warrior and support him in successfully fulfilling his military mission in wartime and peacetime. No matter the man's rank, time in service, or job specialty, fulfilling his part of the overall military mission was everything. Strict adherence to, and total compliance with, the standards of duty, honor, and dedicated service to country superseded any family needs, large or small. The real woman was expected to serve her country and fulfill her part of the mission. That meant picking up the slack on the home front and not bothering her military man with "trivial" domestic details. She was expected to bear, nurture, and raise future male warriors, while teaching her daughters to care for and support the future male warriors they would marry.

So when my brother joined the Army in 1977, it was an expected turn of events. Like my father, he would become one of those warriors who would be on the front line during a conflict. However, I signed up for the two-year Air Force ROTC program at Central Washington University in 1978 and became the sole female member of Air Force ROTC Detachment 895. Several family members and friends were surprised and expressed concern about this decision. Had I taken leave of my military real woman senses and home training? Finally, after one year in the program, it was becoming clear that, as a woman, I would probably never see the front line. That quieted some of the concerns. When I became a commissioned Air Force officer in 1980, the American public's attitude about women serving in combat had not changed significantly from the one I was taught while growing up.

One decade later, however, more than forty thousand servicewomen successfully deployed in support of Operation Desert Storm. When thirteen women were killed and two became POWs during that conflict, the public's views began to change. In response, the Department of Defense, Congress, and the Executive Branch conducted several hearings and ordered investigative studies to analyze how well women performed during the war. Based on the findings, in early 1993 Congress eliminated the combat exclusion policy for women. That allowed women to fly combat aircraft and serve on all surface ships. In 2012, the first group of women was allowed to serve on submarines. Also in 1993, Secretary of Defense Les Aspin revoked the "risk rule," a 1988 Bush Administration mandate that kept women from serving in military jobs that could involve them in direct or even indirect combat. That rule's revocation allowed servicewomen to serve in all types of jobs. They still were excluded from duties that involved engaging in ground combat. Neither could they serve in direct combat areas where engaging the enemy was a high probability, for example, in infantry, armor, and artillery units.

A decade after those sweeping changes, the question of whether women should be in combat is becoming moot, especially in light of what happened to the three women of the 507th. Shortly after the ambush, *Washington Post* columnist Anne Applebaum declared, "The argument about women in combat is over. Women are engaging the enemy in Iraq and American civilization has not collapsed as a result."[2] The combat exploits of Lynch, Johnson, and Piestewa—unintentional though they were—helped lay the foundation for a new twenty-first-century female warrior icon. Their personal stories of military service and sacrifice became ripe pickings for eager Department of Defense image shapers and equally eager national media. A plethora of "women at war" stories were generated, featuring young servicewomen who courageously fought and even died for their country, just as did their male counterparts.

As I watched their stories begin to unfold in the media, I was certain the exploits of the three young Army women had forever changed the public's view of the gender face of war. I felt Shoshana Johnson's story would prove to be especially significant, primarily because of her enormous historical significance as the first African American female POW. As a retired public affairs officer who had served in the Gulf in 1991, my professional military public relations sense recognized that Shoshana's newly acquired place in military history constituted a good story. I was absolutely unprepared, however, for how the stories of Jessica Lynch and Shoshana Johnson played out in the media and how Lori Piestewa was ignored. The coverage exposed media bias, especially regarding race and gender.

To assert that coverage of Private Jessica Lynch was totally out of proportion and misreported and that Shoshana's time as a POW received little interest is not to demean the serious injuries and sexual assault visited upon Jessica. She spent years trying to set the record straight. Nor is it to suggest that government and the media were racially motivated, except that they manufactured a heroine story around an attractive, white girl, plucked from torture by the efforts of heroic male Special Forces. Consciously or not, a fictionalized white girl was deemed to be more appealing and impactful than a significant story of the first African American female POW.

What follows is a lengthy recounting of the government/media coverage of Jessica's capture and rescue and the scandal that eventually erupted out of it. This may seem to drift from the subject of this book. I include it because I think it suggests more clearly than I could about America's attitude toward women in combat generally and African American women soldiers in combat in particular.

Of the two surviving female POWs, Jessica was the first released from captivity. On the evening of April 1, 2003, breaking news reports announced that Jessica had been rescued from an Iraqi hospital by U.S. Special Forces. Since she was the first U.S. female POW rescued by American forces from behind enemy lines, the news captivated the media and their audiences worldwide. The impact of the first photos of a wan, gaunt, and helpless Jessica, draped in an American flag and carried on a stretcher by Special Forces men, were powerful. They were, in fact, eerily reminiscent of photos of severely wounded, emaciated, sunken-faced male Vietnam War POWs returned to U.S. soil. The rescue video, shown worldwide, was cinematically compelling.

Not everyone was moved by the positive imagery of the media coverage. The Project for Excellence in Journalism of the Columbia University Graduate School of Journalism studied Jessica Lynch post-rescue coverage. The analysis questioned the Pentagon's timing of the release of the video and photos. These images just happened to become available at a time when American public opinion about the war had begun to turn.

Christian Science Monitor political columnist Dante Chinni outlined several events that no doubt affected the timing of the release by Pentagon officials:

> Not quite two weeks into the war in Iraq, some of the media's coverage of the fighting had taken a negative turn. In the newspapers and on television, experts were beginning to question whether the United States had sent sufficient manpower to handle the Iraqis, who were fighting harder and more cagily than expected. So were some senior commanders in the field. Defense Secretary Rumsfeld complained about "media mood swings." Peter Arnett, who was appearing on NBC and MNSBC, went on Iraqi television and claimed the U.S. had underestimated the forces they were up against and were having to redraw their battle plans.[3]

Hours after Jessica's much heralded rescue, the media coverage reflected a dramatic upswing in the mood about the war. Buoyed by the photos and video, news reports about Jessica's "fight to the death to avoid being captured" in the 507th's ambush flooded the press. Her story became the first big "feel good" story about Operation Iraqi Freedom and catapulted her to celebrity status as a military hero.

Over the months that followed, Jessica was prominently featured in many favorable prime-time media stories. Typically, the media cast her as the Army's consummate GI Jane, a petite female military fighting machine, a cute but tough-as-nails commando, and the ultimate "Army of One" servicewoman. With great fanfare, she was introduced to viewers and readers via prime-time radio and television shows and national magazine and newspaper articles as an attractive, model-thin, blonde and blue-eyed, small-town West Virginia girl who had aspirations of using her military educational benefits to become a kindergarten teacher. To the Pentagon's public relations gurus, she was publicity gold, her story the epitome of every military recruitment poster, TV and radio commercial message, and movie for which one could only dream.

With her newly sculpted image as a military hero expertly unveiled to a proud and grateful American public, the media could not get or disseminate enough stories about Jessica, the rescued female POW. Those upbeat human-interest portrayals neatly juxtaposed with the front-page hard news stories that morphed Jessica into a M16-wielding Ramboette who fiercely mounted her own one-woman assault on ambushing enemy forces, wounding and killing several hapless foes until her ammunition was spent, and she was critically wounded.

There was just one problem with these and similar versions of the Ramboette stories: They were not true.

Washington Post reporters Vernon Loeb and Dana Priest were later blamed for start the Lynch myth. Their first story on April 2, though, accurately reported the basic facts in the first story about Private Lynch's release from captivity.[4] Citing anonymous senior Pentagon officials, they simply reported on the midnight rescue from the hospital by Special Forces soldiers after CIA operatives pinpointed her location. However, follow-up stories by *The Post* and other media outlets quickly became more sensationalistic and inaccurate. Again citing anonymous military officials, they reported that Jessica had suffered one gunshot wound or had been shot multiple times. Other media accounts stated that she had been stabbed and shot. Still others reported that she had been tortured and abused while held in the Iraqi hospital.

Once the actual nature of Jessica's injuries and her true role in the ambush were revealed, these media outlets had to backtrack and even refute the facts in coverage. She had not been stabbed or shot. She actually suffered two spinal fractures, nerve damage, and a shattered right arm, right foot, and left leg. Her injuries were serious. She was left with no feeling in her left leg below the knee. She still wears a brace so she can walk and stand. She also still suffers from severe bladder and kidney problems. Military doctors who treated her at Landstuhl Regional Medical Hospital in Germany and Walter Reed Army Hospital in Washington, D.C., ultimately determined that she had been sexually assaulted at some point during her captivity. There was no evidence that she had otherwise been tortured or mistreated by Iraqi soldiers or hospital staff.

In 2007, the finger pointing between the military and the media about who misrepresented and manipulated details about Jessica's story became increasingly contentious. Angry media representatives blasted the Defense Department for duping them and a trusting American public with manufactured information. Military representatives blamed the media for relying on unnamed military sources and flawed intelligence reports. Military spokesmen charged that the desire for higher Nielson ratings and Pulitzer Prize nominations had caused the media to generate sensational stories about a media war darling that their own organizations had helped create. When the inaccurate stories about Jessica first surfaced, Pentagon officials claimed, they had tried to set the record straight, but reporters continued producing and running sensational stories.

As the media and the military traded accusations, the public, and later Congress, became outraged by these inaccurate stories. Answers were demanded, especially when it was revealed that yet another story of a war hero had been misrepresented. Early accounts reported that former NFL football player Pat Tillman had been killed by enemy fire in combat in Afghanistan. It turned out that Corporal Tillman of the Army Rangers had actually been killed by the "friendly fire" of other American soldiers. His family appeared before the U.S. House of Representatives Committee on Oversight and Government Reform on April 17, 2007, to testify about the military's misrepresentation of facts to them and the media about the nature of their son's death.

Jessica Lynch was also invited to appear. When she appeared before the committee, Jessica said she wanted to set the record straight about her role in the ambush and rescue. She also wanted to tell how the Pentagon's and national media's insistence on turning her into a wartime hero had caused her and her family to suffer as they were subjected to the public spotlight.

America has remained enthralled with Jessica. Years later she related that people were still asking for her autograph and sending letters, despite all of the reporting of allegations of military spin run amok and media manipulation. She unwillingly became a new symbol of how war claims its victims in a variety of ways.

During a discussion of the topic "Did Media Help Administration Push War Agenda?" on *Fox News Watch*, journalism ethics scholar Jane Hall asserted that Jessica's story shows that the creation of wartime heroes is the work of many culprits. Besides the administration's obvious penchant for manufacturing heroes, Hall said, "the media have a need, the people have a need for heroes, and Jessica is a woman who fit the bill."[5]

Severely injured in the line of duty, her life improvement goals temporarily derailed, Jessica became a hero, but not in the conventional sense. Communication scholars John Howard and Laura Prividera argue that the crux of Jessica's heroine status really centered on how well she played out her role as a defenseless female victim, irrevocably damaged by the ravages of a patriarchal war. The researchers claimed that, in America's eyes, Jessica became "a hapless victim, small, injured, and in pain. In short, Jessica was not fighting for us; Jessica Lynch was what we were fighting for. Media constructed her as a hero but only because she was a victim. . . . Her heroism is for surviving, not for succeeding. She is a hero, not for saving others, but for living to be saved."[6]

For this she was victimized on the home front. That was the price paid for Jessica to became Operation Iraqi Freedom's earliest publicity main course, carved and served up on a platter of battlefield misinformation by overzealous military and media spinmeisters. They were desperate to put a woman's face on heroic military acts, even if it meant fabricating them. As syndicated columnist Cal Thomas noted at the time of the hearings in April, 2007, Jessica's life and reported war exploits became a "template" for creating "the Amazon warrior, the female tough girl." Jessica, however, despised the template's trappings. She became emotionally conflicted, frustrated, and angry at being exploited for the sake of advancing and publicizing a war. Jessica told the congressional committee that was holding hearings on the Tillman scandal:

> I have repeatedly said when asked that if the stories about me helped inspire
> our troops and rally a nation, then perhaps there was some good. However, I
> am still confused as to why they chose to lie and tried to make me a legend
> when the real heroics of my fellow soldiers that day were in fact legendary. . . .
> The bottom line is the American people are capable of determining their own
> ideals for heroes and they don't need to be told elaborate tales.[7]

Despite the finger-pointing and denials emanating from the government and the media about their levels of involvement, Jessica Lynch's launch into prime-time warrior celebrity status would not have been remotely possible unless both entities had tacitly decided to work together on at least some level to create, sustain, and control such an image.

David Ansen suggested in a *Newsweek* story that Jessica's experience is hardly unusual; in fact, it is historically commonplace. Elaborating, Ansen stated:

> The practice of turning wartime exploits into convenient fictions (or warriors
> into gods) is hardly a recent invention. There's the Iliad for one. But Achilles,
> as far as we know, did not have PR handlers. The great American country boy
> celebrity of World War I, Alvin York, was a true hero, but his sharpshooting
> exploits were widely embellished in serialized magazine articles. (It's no coin-
> cidence that when Gary Cooper immortalized him in 1941's *Sergeant York*, we
> were on the brink of another war.) The deeper into the bloody century we
> went—as photography, film, and television increasingly entered into the equa-
> tion—the more inextricably the war machine and the public relations machine
> became entwined.[8]

JESSICA'S ASCENT TO HEROISM

Who determines who becomes a celebrated American war hero or heroine? As noted, Shoshana Johnson story never received the acclaim Jessica's did, even though Shoshana spent a longer time in captivity in much more danger- ous surroundings and conditions. She was released April 14, 2003, with her four male colleagues, after being rescued by the Marines. During her twenty- two-day captivity, her Iraqi captors moved the POWs several times to avoid detection. Shoshana was kept isolated in a separate cell until a few days before her captivity ended. Like Jessica, Shoshana was injured during the ambush. She was shot in both ankles and suffered damage to her right Achilles heel.

As I already noted, I expected Shoshana to receive at least as much media coverage as Jessica, given her story as the first African American female

POW. However, my faith in the media's ability to recognize and promote a newsworthy story quickly gave way to grave doubt and stunned disbelief. Jessica continued to receive a deluge of national media coverage, while Shoshana received a miniscule amount of attention. The media were noticeably silent about her, apart from news coverage of her release from captivity, her reunion with her family and young daughter, and some additional interviews with family members and a few friends.

Finally, African American media outlets, the Black Congressional Caucus, and other prominent African American public figures called attention to the gross inequity in media coverage. The inequity became less pronounced but did not abate. Seven months after her capture, NBC made *Saving Jessica Lynch*, a movie about her capture and rescue. Jessica also received a million-dollar book deal for her autobiography, *"I Am a Soldier Too": The Jessica Lynch Story,*[9] co-authored by Pulitzer Prize winner Rick Bragg. Shoshana did not receive a made-for-TV movie deal. She did get the opportunity to go to New York City and drop the Times Square ball to bring in the 2004 New Year. Kensington Press originally scheduled her book, *One Wrong Turn,* for release in May 2007. Shortly before the book's release date, however, Kensington cancelled her contract, claiming "photo release clearance issues." Kensington executives also asked Shoshana to return the advance they had given her. Shoshana said the publishing company was not interested in her telling her story. They instead demanded that she write a book detailing her personal relationships and conversations with Jessica Lynch and Lori Piestewa. Seven years after she was a POW, Johnson finally got to have her story published in the 2010 release, *I'm Still Standing.*[10]

Clearly, Jessica, Lori, and Shoshana all deserve to have their stories truthfully told. They served their country well. Their great personal sacrifice will forever affect the mental, physical, and emotional lives of Jessica and Shoshana. Lori deserves to receive her just due as the first Native American U.S. Army service woman POW. Her story should be more than a military history footnote.

Several salient questions about the nature of the coverage of these heroic women remain unanswered. Why was Jessica the one characterized in media accounts as a machine-gun-wielding Ramboette? She did not fire a single shot with her M-16 rifle because it jammed, nor did she directly engage the enemy during the ambush. Military reports and Shoshana's own statements in her few media interviews relate that Shoshana managed to get off one round from her M-16 before it jammed. Iraqi soldiers pummeled her with fists and rifle butts before they discovered she was a woman. If that is the case, then why did Jessica become the female poster model for Operation Iraqi Freedom, rather than Shoshana or Lori?

Answers to these complex questions may be found by looking more closely, into why the predominantly white American media and public were not willing to embrace or relate to Shoshana, an unmarried African American single mother whose family had emigrated from Panama. Certainly, her short, stocky body and her cornrows and dark skin contrasted unfavorably with Jessica's lean and petite body and her long blonde hair and pale skin. Lori's biographical pedigree was equally incompatible. She was a divorced single mother, a Native American Hopi tribe member with Hispanic heritage who hailed from a reservation in Tuba City, Arizona.

Given the choice among these three women, the U.S. government and media obviously decided to elevate Jessica's Northern European descended features and persona to provide a more palatable, puritanical heroine's image that white America could readily relate to. According to *New Zealand Herald* columnist Deborah Orr, the rest of the world also readily bought into this image. In that light, Orr suggests that the blonde-haired Jessica, a picture perfect Hollywood media product, became the ". . . archetype of what an All American girl is always portrayed as being . . . so typical of the American ideal . . . America does have a hierarchy of life with pretty blondes at the top, black Americans and native Americans further down and the rest of the world trailing hopelessly…"[11]

Shoshana and Lori had a less desirable U.S. servicewoman's image, what Gary Younge of the U.K.'s newspaper, *The Guardian*, described in April 2003 as ". . . the other American face of this war, fought by a military whose ranks have been swelled by poor, nonwhite women . . ."[12] Specifically citing the different media treatment Jessica and Shoshana received, sociologist Rudolph Alexander contends that this historical pattern of government and media promoting white war heroes over the heroic acts of African American war heroes is "subtle racism." Alexander explains how African Americans in the military have been slighted:

> African Americans do not begrudge Jessica the attention and financial rewards that she has received but criticize the White media and the White Public for ignoring Shoshana Johnson. . . . Jessica Lynch represents a pattern of highlighting White achievements whether true or false and ignoring African Americans. Teddy Roosevelt became a household name when he was shown to have charged up San Juan Hill, but few history books and newspaper drawings show pictures of the Buffalo Soldiers going up San Juan Hill too, alongside Teddy Roosevelt and his Rough Riders.[13]

At a March 23, 2007, memorial service for Lori Piestewa in Phoenix, Arizona, Shoshana sat next to Jessica. According to Shoshana, several of the media outlets that covered the event ignored her and the other attendees and focused on Jessica. Shoshana's image was even edited out of newspaper photos and broadcast video coverage. Such slights clearly took their toll on Shoshana, as she shared in a National Public Radio interview: "It hurts, you know. I contributed to my government and to my country, and it's hard when your contribution is ignored. You know, when they act like you don't exist. And I definitely know if I feel like that, I can't imagine how my male counterparts feel, because they are completely ignored."[14]

As I pondered Shoshana's admission of feeling hurt because of the media's maltreatment, I wondered whether other black women soldiers have been ignored in similar ways. If her story was not considered worthy of national media coverage, what about the stories of other black women who have served this country in wartime, particularly in the Gulf? With that Iraqi grainy video image of Shoshana seared indelibly in my mind, I lamented the disparity in coverage. Colleagues and friends began to urge me to conduct research that could be published to examine the issue publicly. Perhaps I could bring to the forefront some of the Gulf War's untold "herstories" of African American military servicewomen.

The result is this book, which is built upon one central premise: Since the American Revolution, African American women have served, usually behind the scene, in every military conflict in which the United States has been engaged. Despite this dedicated service to their country, very little empirical research has been published regarding African American servicewomen, including those who have served in the Gulf wars (Operation Desert Storm and Operation Iraqi Freedom). There has been a decided lack of interest among the national media's on the accomplishments of African American military women. The story of Shoshana is an example of the disparity in media coverage. These oversights could be rectified to some extent by giving a voice in print to African American servicewomen's stories. Interviews and oral histories provide this voice, as well as in the soldiers' written documents. Autobiographical narratives can compile a significant African American and women's military history reservoir. One benefit of such a reservoir is that the servicewomen themselves can dip into the soothing waters of their own military accomplishments and the stories of others.

Therefore, the most important feature in the following chapters will be the stories of black women, who candidly and poignantly share their war experiences. Their stories resonate with the experiences of other African American women in military conflict. We will look at the varied facets of professional, sociological, and interpersonal experience among a group of black women in the two Gulf Wars. Those facets include such issues as health care, childcare, sexism and sexual harassment, racism, religion, promotions, and career advancement, as well as combat. The accounts related by these women fit alongside experiences of other African American women and others who serve or have served.

METHODOLOGY

Communication research methodologist Robert Bostrom says that, when scholars are faced with trying to find answers to pressing research problems, they must determine the absolute best strategy to solve the empirical puzzle. In the end, I decided that a hybrid oral history/narrative chronicle would best fit the bill to capture the stories effectively. As feminist oral historians Dana Jack and Kathryn Anderson explained,

> Oral history interviews provide an invaluable means of generating new insight about women's experiences in their worlds. The spontaneous exchange within an interview offers possibilities of freedom and flexibility for researchers and narrators alike. For the narrator, the interview provides the opportunity to tell her own story in her own terms. For researchers, taped interviews preserve living treasure for present and future use; we can rummage through interviews as we do an old attic-probing, comparing, checking insights, find new treasures the third time through, then arranging and carefully documenting our thoughts. [15]

Oral history scholar Rebecca Sharpless relates that oral history is a time-honored method of gathering, processing, and preserving history. She points out that, before history was preserved in written form, it was gathered and saved orally. The Greeks used first-person oral history accounts, collected from their warriors, to document fifth century BCE battles of the Persian Wars. For more than seven centuries, West African griots or storytellers have served as oral history gatherers and chroniclers of African kings, nations, and villages. Noted for their mastery of music and compelling and creative verbal agility, griots have used a unique style of sharing and preserving oral history. They combine lengthy genealogy recitations, composing and singing ballads, and dispensing cultural wisdom and traditions through poetry and proverbs to meld the past with the present. [16]

The United States has known sweeping social and cultural changes. Two of the more recent are the 1960s Civil Rights Movement and the 1970s Women's Movement. A wide variety of racial and social groups and organizations have begun using oral history to document and preserve the contributions to society of those who participated in these times. Through oral narratives, Rebecca Sharpless notes, social and cultural changes can be examined and used to successfully challenge the more traditional chronicles that highlight those with elite status. Outlining the significance of this challenge, Mary Larson said that

> the civil rights movement, protests against the Vietnam War and the feminist movement all raised questions about American history based on the deeds of elite White men. Contesting the status quo, social historians began to explore

the interests of multiracial, multiethnic population with an emphasis on class relationships. As they sought to understand the experiences of ordinary people, historians turned to new ways of discovering the pluralistic mind of the nation.[17]

Naturally there have been, and still are, traditional historians who eschew this user-friendly approach to handling history. Barbara Tuchman and Nathan Reingold are two prominent historians who argue that oral history is prone to dubious reliability because untrained, amateur historians so frequently are the ones who conduct interviews. Reingold in particular raises tough questions regarding validity and reliability. Such academic criticism has forced historians who defend this type of history to establish and standardize credible research boundaries. Establishment of American Oral History and International Oral History associations helped to build a regulatory infrastructure that provided legal and empirical guidelines, research models, and interviewing standards for oral history gathering, collecting, and archiving. Questions and concerns still surface periodically from critical historians, but the plethora of well-researched and documented projects by scholars and laypersons has quieted most criticism.

In structuring the oral history process and focus for this book, I picked the subject-oriented oral history style. This approach allows me to take a broad approach when examining the extent to which the history of African American servicewomen has been historically chronicled, while allowing me to recount some stories to add to this history. To supplement my oral history interview method, I conducted my research using the grounded theory "inductive approach" of Barney Glaser and Anselm Straus, gathering, handling (coding), and processing the data I collected from the interviews.[18]

Using grounded theory as a guide, I took two key steps while gathering the data and compiling the research to design my research framework: First, I ensured that those who were a part of this study's sample had experienced the research problem first hand. All the women I interviewed have served either in one of the Gulf conflicts. One woman served in both. All of these women served directly in the Southwest Asia Theater. Second, using grounded theory, I made sure that both academicians and laypersons can easily understand the research process and results. By using the stories provided by the interviewees and explaining military acronyms or other terms not readily known to civilian audiences, I was able to meet that challenge.

Since these oral histories are personal stories shared in individual ways by the women interviewed, the content is wholly intimate and revealing. Their stories fit their own particular situation and time period of military service. These are not every African American servicewoman's Gulf wars story, but many who served will no doubt relate to the events and situations.

Finally, the telling of these women's stories can serve as the consummate launch pad for convincing scholars that more such accounts should be preserved. As Brown University scholar Tricia Rose has suggested, "it is crucial to have access to more stories by Black women, told in such a way that they not only illuminate the lives and social forces that shape them but also allow a given story's messy seams to show, let the many life threads that run through them remain visible."[19]

HANDLING OUR HISTORY: GATHERING STORIES OF AFRICAN AMERICAN GULF WARS SERVICEWOMEN

African American women leaders have strongly advocated collecting and maintaining their own histories. In her 1892 book, *A Voice from the South,* African American feminist and historian Anna Julia Cooper told African American women that they needed to gather their history. They should then muster the creativity and ingenuity to develop and cultivate their own collective literary and rhetorical voice. Cooper's fundamental fear was that individual and collective life stories and experiences would be ignored and totally dismissed by white men and women, as well as by African American men. A century later, feminist bell hooks echoed Cooper's admonition and urged African American women to speak up and out about themselves and their lives. Doing so would avoid having their histories and life experiences deemed insignificant or rendered invisible.

Traditionally, African American women of all ages and backgrounds have looked for such a collective voice. That voice has been found in preserving history through the telling and the passing on of their stories. African American women are no strangers to storytelling, because significant storytelling goes on within the African American community. Not everyone can tell the story. African American women want someone they can trust, someone who will understand them well enough to tell their story and articulate their concern from their own perspective.

As an African American woman who served in the first Gulf War, I felt I could properly share the stories. I began with a national search for interviewees. I tried to get as wide a variety of women from the various military services as possible, so I sought those in active duty, veterans, and reservists with the National Guard, Army, Navy, Marines, and Air Force. I specifically wanted to interview women who had actually served in the regions where the conflicts occurred. I felt they would have a different perspective of their role in the war if they had actually left the United States or Europe to experienced war first hand. I wrote to forty-five national military organizations and to email discussion groups, asking that they pass along news about my search for interviewees in their newsletters and online. I received more than two

hundred initial inquiries from women who had personally served in Desert
Shield, Desert Storm, or Operation Iraqi Freedom or who knew of someone
who had.

I sent a brief questionnaire to interested parties, seeking basic biographical and military service information (e.g., name, rank, job specialty, and time
and place of service in the Gulf region). I also asked some open-ended
questions about experiences regarding health care, child care, racism, sexism,
and sexual harassment. The questionnaire was my preliminary screening tool
to determine which stories I would gather. Each potential interviewee received a packet of information that outlined the book's purpose and provided
them with a chapter synopsis. Once I selected the interviewees, I worked
with them to determine interview times and to clear up any questions they or
I might have. Since interviewees lived all over the country, I conducted taped
phone interviews that lasted from a half-hour to one hour. Because of the
nature of war, some had suffered trauma and other bad experiences associated with their service. I was careful to let them know that they could answer
as many or as few of my questions as they wanted. I did not want to make
anyone feel uncomfortable.

In addition to the questionnaire responses, I developed twenty to twenty-
five additional open-ended follow-up questions. Each interviewee had the
option to identify herself by real name and military unit or to use a pseudo-
nym.

The interviews were surprisingly personal. These women came ready to
tell their stories. I did not have to pry or prod. I was amazed at how much of
their lives they shared. At times during interviews, I laughed or cried with
them. Some said that the interview time was cathartic.

Most of the women interviewed were enlisted personnel. I interviewed
two officers. One commanded a Civil Engineer's Squadron in Operation
Iraqi Freedom. The other was a company commander of an Army administrative unit in Desert Storm. The woman who served in both conflicts was
first a junior enlisted Air Force member and later a senior noncommissioned
officer. One was among the first woman aircraft fuel technicians in the Air
Force. She served with an AWACS unit in Desert Storm that also included
her husband. One interviewee drove a large vehicle down the infamous
"Highway of Death" connecting Kuwait and Iraq, the scene of bloody battles.
Another interviewee arrived in Iraq around the time Shoshanna's unit was
captured. She went through the same horror of briefly being in a lost Army
convoy as she drove a jeep for her company commander and two other
passengers.

Several of the women were forced to leave their children behind with
family and friends. These stories are especially heart-rending, especially in
the children's reactions to their departures and returns. Four women were
married to active duty personnel deployed in Desert Storm at the same time.

The threat of death was a constant fear. One of the interviewees was in the barracks that was bombed before Desert Storm officially ended. Some continue to suffer from PTSD. A few have from mild to severe Gulf War syndrome symptoms.

Without exception, each interviewee felt that stories about African American women's service in the Gulf wars should be told in order to preserve a valuable history. They wanted to dispel stereotypes about black women not being hard working and patriotic. While several of them were surprised that I would find their stories compelling, they were glad someone was attempting to relate their experiences. It surprised me to learn that not one of them regretted her service and would serve again if asked.

Chapter two, "Why We Serve: An Historical Overview of African American Women's Military Service from the Revolutionary War Through the Gulf Wars," presents a chronological synopsis of African American women's service in various conflicts, from the American Revolutionary War to the present. Chapter three, "Sistahs of Defense: Duties and Dangers of African American Women in Service in the Gulf Wars," shows the wide variety of military duties undertaken by African American servicewomen and the dangers faced. Three African American servicewomen died in Operation Desert Shield/ Desert Storm. Twenty six military and civilian African American women died in Operation Iraqi Freedom. Army Specialist Shoshana Johnson became the first African American female prisoner of war.

Chapter four, "My Child Left Behind: The Family and Child Care Challenges Faced by African American Gulf War Servicewomen," discusses family separation issues. Chapter 5, "What Happens in the Desert Stays in the Desert: African American Women Confront Racism and Sexism in the Gulf," looks at Gulf War experiences with racism, sexism and sexual harassment. Chapter six, "Where My Health Comes From: African American Servicewomen Battle Gulf War Illnesses," looks at a host of health issues faced, including pregnancy, post-traumatic stress disorder, and Gulf War syndrome. The epilogue, "Marching as to War: Final Thoughts," addresses the need for further research and more stories to be told and published.

Segments of some stories will be referred to in more than one chapter. I begin each chapter with a brief autobiographical narrative of my own deployment in Operation Desert Storm that fits with the chapter's focus.

It is my hope that this work will make its way into mainstream collections of military oral histories so that narratives like these and the stories of many other African American servicewomen who served in the Gulf Wars can finally receive the recognition and the voice they deserve.

NOTES

1. U.S. Army, "Official Report on the 507th Maintenance Co.: An Nasiriyah, Iraq." Accessed at www.why-war.com/files/article07102003a.pdf.

2. Quoted by Kate Obeirne in "A New Horror of War," *National Review*, 55.7 (21 April 2003), 24.

3. Dante Chinni, "Jessica Lynch: Media Myth-Making in the Iraq War," Website of the Project for Excellence in Journalism, Pew Research Center, June 23, 2003, 1. Accessed at www.journalism.org/node/223.

4. Henry Waxman, statement in U.S. House of Representatives hearing of the Committee for Oversight and Government Reform, April 24, 2007. Accessed at http:www.//oversight-archive.waxman.house.gov/story.asp?ID=1266.

5. Jane Hall, addressing the question, "Did Media Help Administration Push War Agenda?" *Fox News Watch* interview, April 18, 2007.

6. John W. Howard III and Laura C. Prividera, "Rescuing Patriarchy or Saving 'Jessica Lynch': The Rhetorical Construction of the American Woman Solider," *Women and Language*, 27.2, 89–101.

7. Jessica Lynch, "Opening Statement before House of Representatives Committee for Oversight and Government Reform," video tape uploaded on YouTube, April 24, 2007. Accessed at http://www.youtube.com/watch?v=l0OyihqYfF4.

8. David Ansen, "Inside the Hero Factory," *Newsweek* 148.17 (23 October, 2006), 70–71.

9. Jessica Lynch, *I Am a Soldier Too: The Jessica Lynch Story* (New York: Vintage, 2004).

10. Shoshana Johnson and M.L. Doyle, *I'm Still Standing: From Captive U.S. Soldier to Free Citizen—My Journey Home* (New York: Touchstone, 2011).

11. Quoted by Antonia Zerbisias, *Toronto Star*, April 6, 2003. Accessed at www.commondreams.org/views03/0406-04.htm.

12. Gary Younge, *The Guardian*, London, April 2003.

13. Rudolph Alexander, *Racism, African Americans, and Social Justice* (Lanham, MD.: Rowman & Littlefield, 2005), 70–71.

14. From a National Public Radio report, "Life After Iraq," May 28, 2007. Accessed at www.npr.org/templates/story/story.php?storyId=10495193.

15. Kathryn Anderson and Dana C. Jack, "Learning to Listen: Interview Techniques and Analyses," in *Women's Words: The Feminist Practice of Oral History,* edited by Sherna Gluck and Daphne Patai (New York: Routledge, 1991), 11.

16. Thomas L. Charlton, Lois Meyers, and Rebecca Sharpless, *Handbook of Oral History* (Lanham, MD.: Altamira, 2006).

17. Ibid, 24.

18. Barney Glaser and Anselm Strauss, *The Discovery of Grounded Theory: Strategies for Qualitative Research* (Chicago: Aldine, 1967).

19. Tricia Rose, *Longing to Tell: The Sexual Lives of Black Women, in Their Own Words* (New York: Farrar, Straus and Giroux, 2003).

Chapter Two

Why We Serve

An Historical Overview of
African American Women's Military Service
from the Revolutionary War through the Gulf Wars

And even I can remember a day when the historians left blanks in their writings, I mean for things they did not know.
—Ezra Pound, poet and social critic

When I talk to students, they say, "How did it feel to know you were making history?" But you don't know you're making history when it's happening; I just wanted to do my job."
—Lt. Col. Charity Adams Earley, commander 6888th Battalion, Central Postal Direction, World War II

As a third-generation military service member, I grew up treasuring military history, especially as it pertained to African Americans. I devoted fifteen years to Air Force service, honoring the significance of traditions. My step-grandfather served in the Army during World War II, and my father joined the Army shortly after the Korean War ended.

From my earliest days, I had a legacy and a foundation to build upon. I began building early. In elementary school, I would incessantly beg my parents for permission to take to school any piece of my father's uniform or military paraphernalia for show and tell. I wanted to show things that illustrated his Army duties. I was a big hit in fourth grade when I brought his gas mask to class and demonstrated how to use it properly. That same year, I was a hit once again when I wore some of his colorful military ribbons and medals on my blouse, accompanied by one of his khaki Army caps, cocked jauntily on the side of my head.

I cultivated the second phase of nurturing my military heritage by attending countless Department of Defense "show-and-tell" events. I grew up participating in a plethora of military activities, which were specifically designed to help maintain and pass on military traditions to succeeding generations. These were meant to instill pride for the Army's mission in youthful hearts and awe over the military strength of the United States. For me, this strategy worked. I was enthralled. I rarely missed a military parade or a change of command ceremony, no matter what Army post I lived on as a child or which Air Force base I was assigned to as an adult. It was mesmerizing to watch young men and women, marching in synchronized, vocally commanded rhythm, past review stands crowded with high-ranking military and civilian dignitaries.

I spent annual Army post open houses climbing in and out of tanks and helicopters with my brother and sister, running our hands admiringly over the equipment in a large arsenal of artillery and aircraft weaponry. My father's annual unit Family Day picnics taught me first-hand about the awesomeness of the continental air defense capability of the Nike-Hercules missile. Knowing that my father's duties supported a military weapon that was touted as the "last continental bastion of defense" made my two siblings and I feel safe and proud.

As I grew older, I underwent phases of military history and heritage bonding. As a teen, I read as many military history books, magazine articles, and news articles as I could get my hands on during weekly treks to libraries. As a young twenty-something adult, I spent my most enjoyable times gathering military history. During my fifteen-year career as an Air Force public affairs officer, I listened and talked to some of the older male, and occasionally female, African American veterans of the world wars, Korea, and Vietnam. I considered those veterans to be interactive, living military history.

A high point of this work of gathering veterans' narratives came in 1993. I had the opportunity to meet U.S. Air Force General Benjamin Davis Jr., the first African American to become a general in the Air Force, and members of his famed African American World War II 332nd Fighter Group, the Tuskegee Airmen. Davis coolly recounted how he survived four years of "silencing," an old West Point cadet practice of shunning peers who violated or were accused of violating the Point's honor code. The silencing ploy was designed to demoralize him, break his will, and drive him from the academy. During the four years at West Point, he ate alone and roomed alone. His classmates and instructors spoke to him only when necessary for official academy business. Despite being ostracized, he persevered, graduated, and was commissioned in 1936, thirteenth in a class of 276 cadets. Years after this harsh racist treatment, he noted wryly, some of his Academy classmates steadfastly denied ever silencing Davis, but others apologized.

Listening to or reading the stories of General Davis and other black veterans, I began to notice a common thread through their shared perspectives. From their stories, I learned that the triumphs and pitfalls they experienced during their military service helped them successfully combat fierce racial discrimination and prejudice on global battlefields and the home front. The discipline and drive they developed as fruits of their military service ultimately gave them the strength to come home from war and confront a nation that was neither receptive nor appreciative.

Historian Catherine Clinton's observation about the exploits of such veterans further illuminates that common thread:

> Blacks have fought and died in the Americas for centuries, creating an unbroken chain of warriors stretching back nearly 500 years. African Americans took up arms whenever given the opportunity. . . . They have fought throughout the Americas and beyond America's borders. Black warriors fought for the independence and preservation of the United States. They have risked their lives to secure freedom for their families and their people. Simultaneously Blacks have waged a fierce struggle to be treated with dignity, to be viewed as equals and to be recognized for their valor and achievements. Thus, their accomplishments in the military as patriots and as freedom fighters are too important not to be told.[1]

Only in recent years have national organizations such as Women in Military Service for America Memorial Foundation and the National Association of Black Military Women begun to gather and share similar stories of African American female veterans who have also served in this country's military conflicts.

This chapter offers a chronological synopsis of African American women's service from the American Revolution to the present.

IN WAR, ONLY MEN ARE CREATED EQUAL: AFRICAN AMERICAN WOMEN AND THE AMERICAN REVOLUTION

The central premise of this book is that African American women have always served this country during war and peace time in some capacity. Therefore, it is fitting to begin with their American Revolution service. Colonists had decided a few years before the Declaration of Independence that neither women nor any African Americans would take part as soldiers in any action. Because of Southern opposition to white soldiers serving with African Americans and their fear of having slaves escape or stage insurrections, George Washington initially did not allow black males to enlist in the Continental Army. Washington rescinded that policy when Lord Dunmore, the royal governor of Virginia, in November 1775 offered African American men their freedom if they fought for the British in the governor's all-black Ethiopian Regiment. Thousands of African American male slaves and their spouses fled from their slave masters during the war years and several hundred risked capture and death, to answer Dunmore's call. Some single African American women slaves also ran off from their masters to join the British.[2]

Three years later, white Continental Army soldiers began deserting in droves and other men refused to leave their farms and plantations to help replenish the thinning ranks. Washington asked each colony to allow African Americans to serve in the Continental Army, a military organization that he later dubbed his "mixed multitude."[3] With the enlistment restriction lifted, African Americans soldiers formed their own New England-based regiments, such as the 1st Rhode Island. African American men from every part of the colonies served in the war, most in integrated units.[4] Washington did not promise freedom to African American slaves who served. Several Southern states (e.g., South Carolina) allowed black men to fight in the war under the guise of preserving the new nation but still kept them enslaved.

Despite these restrictions, at the height of the Revolutionary War, African American males constituted 15 percent (approximately five thousand troops) of the Continental Army. African American women, freed and escaped slaves, traveled with these troops. They fed the soldiers, cleaned and sewed their clothes, and took care of the sick, wounded, and dying.[5]

Not all African American women were able to leave the plantations and travel with the black male troops. Some African American female slaves had to remain on the home front to continue their plantation domestic duties and conduct "agricultural labor" duties on behalf of the war. With a severe shortage of available African American male slaves and white male workers, these female slaves also did manual labor. Hine (2005), elaborating on the nature of these duties, stated: "During the sieges of Savannah, Charleston, and other smaller low-country towns, black women were part of the enslaved workforces dispatched to build and repair fortifications."[6]

With the surrender of the English Army at Yorktown in 1781 and the Treaty of Paris in 1783, the colonies were free from British rule, thanks in part to the efforts of African American men and women. However, it would take another war eighty years later before many African Americans would enjoy that same freedom. According to Harriet Beecher Stowe, they "served a nation that did not acknowledge them as citizens and as equals."

NOTHING CIVIL ABOUT WAR: AFRICAN AMERICAN WOMEN HELP HEAL A BROKEN NATION

When most people think of how African American women served in the Civil War, Harriet Tubman, Tubman, also known as "Moses," comes to mind. She was her era's undisputed human escape artist, ultimately helping more than three hundred slaves to flee to freedom through the Underground Railroad. The Underground Railroad was a clandestine system of homes, barns, churches, and underground tunnels, strategically spread throughout the South and North. This network was used by free blacks and white abolitionist sympathizers to hide escaped slaves from bounty hunters until they could be safely transported to freedom. Tubman, the acknowledged conductor of this symbolic railroad, was a master of disguise and ingenuity. An escaped slave herself, she boldly went into the deepest of Southern slave territories, pulling off daring rescue raids without ever being captured or losing a rescued slave to bounty hunters. In desperation, Confederate slave owners placed a forty-thousand-dollar "dead-or-alive" bounty on her, but that did not deter Tubman from making more than twenty rescue trips to the South.[7] While the South vilified her, Union Army leaders so coveted Tubman's intelligence-gathering acumen and her ability to run a complicated system like the Underground Railroad that they signed her up to work for the Union.

Apparently, Tubman was not content with rescuing slaves or being an elusive Union spy or scout. Historian Lerone Bennett Jr. believes Tubman was the first woman to lead U.S. Army troops in battle. To bolster his claim, Bennett cited part of a newspaper account of a Tubman-led military raid that appeared in the *Boston Commonwealth*, July 10, 1863:

> Colonel Montgomery and his gallant band of 300 Black soldiers, under the guidance of a Black woman, dashed into the enemy's country, struck a bold and effective blow, destroying millions of dollars worth of commissary stores, cotton and lordly dwellings, and striking terror into the hearts of rebeldom, brought off near 800 slaves, and thousands of dollars worth of property, without losing a man or receiving a scratch. It was a glorious consummation.[8]

Tubman was not just a warrior. She also was a self-taught health practitioner, as were other African American women pressed into serving as nurses during the seventeenth and eighteenth and part of the nineteenth centuries. The Union Army praised her for taking care of African American and white male troops while serving as a nurse near the Sea Island South Carolina coast and taking care of black troops at Fort Monroe, Virginia.

However, when Tubman requested a Civil War pension for her own military services as a nurse and scout, she was rebuffed. United States Secretary of State William H. Seward even took up the cause with equally unsuccessful results. She did receive a monthly eight-dollar pension under the Dependent Pension Act of 1890 for being the widow of Nelson Davis, who served in the United States Colored Infantry from 1863 to 1865. In 1897, a bill from the 55th Congress granted a twenty-five-dollar widow's pension to Tubman. However, Tubman was only given twenty dollars monthly until 1913. When Tubman died in 1913 at the age of 101, she was buried with full military honors at Fort Hill Cemetery, Auburn, New York. In 1944, the U.S Navy launched a cargo vessel (liberty ship), *The S.S. Tubman* in her honor. The ship was turned into scrap metal in 1972. In 2002, Senator Hillary Clinton (D-New York) submitted a concurrent congressional resolution proclaiming that ". . . Harriet Tubman should have been paid a pension for her service as a nurse and scout in the United States Army during the Civil War." Senator Clinton's resolution noted that other women who posed as men during the Civil War had received military service pensions.

Closing the loop on Tubman's pension slight, Clinton's submission to the 107th Congress made this declaration:

> *Resolved by the Senate (the House of Representatives concurring),* that—
> (1) Congress recognize that Harriet Tubman served as a nurse and scout in the United States Army during the Civil War; and
> (2) It is the sense of Congress that Harriet Tubman should have been paid a pension at the rate of $25 each month for her service in the United States Army.[9]

On October 29, 2003, Senator Clinton obtained $11,750 through the Senate FY '04 Appropriations Bill for preservation of the Harriet Tubman Home in Auburn, N.Y. These funds are equivalent to the additional amount Tubman should have received in her widow's pension.

Just as during the American Revolutionary War, scores of African American women escaped from plantations and found domestic work with Union Army camps during the Civil War. One of these young women, Susan "Susie" King Taylor, from Georgia, became a Union Army volunteer nurse and traveled with her husband's unit, Company E, 33rd Regiment of the Colored Troops, 1st South Carolina Volunteers, in 1862. Taylor had run away to St. Simons Island at age fourteen. She evidently had received an education, for the young girl soon opened a school for children and adults. She then married and began her Army career.

Although Taylor's official regiment job title was "laundress," she rarely had time to commit herself solely to that duty. Taylor wrote: "I was enrolled as company laundress, but I did very little of it, because I was always busy doing other things through camp, and was employed all the time doing some-thing for the officers and comrades."[10] By necessity, Taylor was pressed into service as a weapons master, loading, firing, and maintaining the regiment's muskets. At times, she even served as a night sentry, guarding against Confederate raids. Taylor also taught some in the regiment to read and write.

Smallpox breakouts were rampant among Union and Confederate soldiers. Besides taking care of the soldiers' sicknesses, she remembered helping doctors take care of some horrific battlefield wounds. She wrote, "We are able to see the most sickening sights, such as men with their limbs blown off and mangled by the deadly shell, without a shoulder; and instead of turning away, how we hurry to assist in alleviating the pain, bind up their wounds and press the cool water to their parched lips."[11]

Despite all of Taylor's dedication to this regiment, the U.S. government never financially compensated her for her volunteer work. Only contract nurses were paid during the war. There is no indication that she was bitter about this treatment. About the service, she "gave at all times for the comfort of the men," Taylor wrote, "I was very happy to know my efforts were successful in camp and also felt grateful for the appreciation of my services. I gave my service for four years and three months without receiving a dollar. I was glad however, to be allowed to go with the regiment to care for the sick and afflicted comrades."[12]

After the death of her husband, Sergeant Edward King, she like Harriet Tubman, collected a widow's pension but also had to work as a teacher and hire herself out as a maid to make ends meet. Taylor was the only African American woman who chronicled her Civil War service with the Union, *Reminiscences of My Life with the 33D United States Colored Troops Late 1st South.Carolina Volunteers,* published in 1902.

Other African American nurses received payment for the services they rendered during the Civil War. From 1863 to 1864, 181 African American male and female nurses did contract work at eleven Union Army hospitals in three states. The female nurses served as part of a women's labor force of twenty thousand, assembled for the Union's relief efforts. African American women constituted 10 percent of this labor force. Carnegie, King, and Schultz have offered a more complete look at this labor pool as a socioeconomic potpourri of the black women's population, with freed and runaway slaves, educated and illiterate.[13]

No matter their social status, many of these women were willing to work alongside white women for little or no pay to help the North win the African Americans' quest for freedom. Schultz provided a numerical breakdown of the duties of 2069 African American women who made up this work force: "Carded service records at the National Archives list 420 nurses (6% of all nurses), 790 matrons or maids of all work (7%), 363 cooks (36%—more than one-third of all cooks), and 309 laundresses (14%). The remaining held jobs in other categories, such as 'dining room girl' or 'chambermaid.'"[14]

The Union Navy also used an African American female labor force. Several of these women served on ships with their husbands and worked in a variety of capacities. King's research dispelled long-held belief that Civil War-era African American women worked only with the Union Army. Eight African American women served aboard the hospital ship U.S.S. Rover as laundresses and nurses. Harriet Ruth (a Navy enlistee) served as a nurse on the U.S.S. Black Hawk with her husband Alfred. Harriet Little, another Navy female enlistee, and her husband Samuel served as nurses on the U.S.S. Hartford. Ann Stokes, who served on the U.S.S. Red Rover, may well be the first woman who was a formal Navy enlistee during the Civil War. In 1890, Stokes applied for and received a pension for her Civil War military service. Lucy Berington, likely an escaped slave, also enlisted in the Navy and served as a laundress for the New Bern, North Carolina, Navy Hospital. [15]

Both Union and Confederate forces ultimately realized the value of African American female labor, but neither side fully documented all of the work provided by these women. Recognizing this oversight, Taylor made a passionate plea in her memoirs for a collective historical accounting of these women's contributions to Civil War efforts:

> There are many people who do not know what some of the colored women did during the war. There were hundreds of them who assisted the Union soldiers by hiding them and helping them to escape. Many were punished for taking food to the prison stockades for the prisoners . . . others assisted in various ways the Union Army. These things should be kept in history before the people. [16]

After the Civil War, all women were still restricted from military service. One African American woman, however, went to extraordinary lengths to serve on the Western frontier with men. In 1866, Congress allowed 12,500 African American men to serve in segregated units, the 9th and 10th Cavalry, and four infantry regiments, the 38th, 39th, 40th, and 41st.

That November in St. Louis, Missouri, twenty-two-year-old former slave Cathay Williams became male soldier William Cathay and joined the Buffalo Soldiers' 38th Infantry Regiment, assigned to Company A. Today, no one knows what she looked like, although most historians describe her as tall (five feet, nine inches) and dark-skinned. Cathay most likely lied about many personal details to get the recruiters to allow her to join the military, so there are very few clues about her background. A few historical accounts claim that Cathay "involuntarily left" the military two years after she became a Buffalo Solider when doctors "accidentally" discovered she was a woman. However, other historians of the Buffalo Soldiers legacy, such as Schubert, contend that Cathay actually fooled everyone throughout her short time of service, even after having repeated military doctor examinations. Originally signed up for a three-year enlistment, Cathay was discharged from the Army on October 14, 1868, at the urging of a military physician, for being incapable of performing her duties. [17]

During her time of service she was hospitalized five times. Like the men assigned to the all-black regiment, Cathay lived the grueling life of a Buffalo Soldier; with constant military drills, scouting for Indians, and garrison duty. At times her unit would march fifty miles to new military post assignments. Only in June 1891, when she applied for a disability pension, did she reveal her true gender and name. The Army ultimately denied her pension request, not because she was a woman, but because it was determined that the ailments she claimed to have suffered as a Buffalo Solider were not connected to military service.[18]

Cathay was most likely the first African American woman to serve in the U.S. Regular Army. After her military discharge she became Cathy Williams again and moved to Fort Union, Colorado, where she worked as a cook. Historical records indicate that she finally settled in Trinidad, Colorado.[19]

FIGHTING FEVER: AFRICAN AMERICAN WOMEN NURSES IN THE SPANISH-AMERICAN WAR

While the all-male Buffalo Soldiers 10th Cavalry charged up San Juan Hill with Theodore Roosevelt in 1898 during the Spanish-American War, African American women once again had to fight their own battle to serve their country. As historian Brenda Moore observed, "African American women have willingly shared the burden of national defense out of a sense of moral obligation to the country but also in an attempt to demonstrate their worthiness for full citizenship. Their efforts were often in vain, however, because the services of women and minorities were forgotten as soon as the conflict was resolved."[20]

Ironically, a racist stereotypical assumption about blacks' physiological makeup eventually allowed some African American women to serve in this conflict. According to M. Elizabeth Carnegie, it was disease, not the Spanish military that killed most American soldiers who fought in Cuba.[21] White female nurses volunteered to serve, but not enough came forward to help stem the ravages of malaria, typhoid fever, and yellow fever. African American women initially were rebuffed when they requested to serve, but the stereotypical belief that all blacks were immune to these types of fevers ultimately opened the door. Namahyoke Curtis (wife of Austin M. Curtis, superintendent-surgical chief of the Washington, D.C., Freedman's Hospital, helped recruit thirty-two African American women nurses. She believed that they, like her, would be "immune" to these fevers. In total, eighty African American women served as nurses during this conflict. Willing to put their lives at risk, they were sent where the epidemics were most severe. Two died of typhoid fever.[22]

ALWAYS THE VOLUNTEER, NEVER THE SOLDIER: AFRICAN AMERICAN WOMEN'S WORLD WAR I SERVICE

As the United States entered World War I, intense pressure emanated from the African American press and other civil rights organizations to allow African American women to serve in the military. Anticipating resistance to their serving as military nurses, African American nurses joined the Red Cross. Carl and Dorothy Schneider suggest that the national racist antipathy to African American women taking care of troops was so pervasive that the Army managed to stave off most of the pressure from the black press and Emmett J. Scott, African American special assistant to the War Department.[23]

The Army made one small compromise, allowing eighteen African American nurses to enter the Army Nurse Corps once the war was over. These nurses went to Camp Grant, Illinois, and Camp Sherman, Ohio, where they were only allowed to care for black male soldiers and German prisoners of war. They were subjected to racial and gender discrimination, lived in substandard segregated housing, and were barred from officers' and enlisted men's clubs. Under threat of courts-martial for insubordination, they involuntarily performed menial cleaning tasks that had nothing to do with their nursing skills. Several of the nurses complained that the German prisoners of war were given more privileges and treated better than they. However, the women decided to stick it out and serve. Their time in service was brief, however. The African American nurses were released from the Army in August of the following year.

African American women who were determined to find other ways to serve their country during the war went overseas to work through the Young Men's Christian Association (YMCA). Prominent social workers Addie Hunton and Kathryn Johnson published a book in 1920 about their service, *Two Colored Women with the Expeditionary Force*.[24] They became Y-secretaries for one hundred fifty thousand African American troops in France. According to their memoir, their job was especially challenging because they had to battle racism and indifference from the U.S. and the YMCA regarding the moral, spiritual, and emotional well-being of African American military men. A year before they had arrived, the first African American woman sent to France by the YMCA had been banned and declared *persona non grata* by U.S. Army officers. Hunton and Johnson acidly observed that these officers "had brought from our southland their full measure of sectional prejudice."[25]

Some white YMCA officials also inflicted their homeland racial views on African American male troops. As a result, these troops could not enter many YMCA facilities. If allowed in, they could use the facilities for only limited hours or receive limited services. Even with limited staff and financial resources, the three women helped African American soldiers fulfill the

YMCA promise to provide wholesome recreation for the American Expeditionary Forces. They helped men to write letters home and taught some to read and write. They served as nurses and cooks. They lent a sympathetic ear to those lonely for someone to talk to and helped conduct religious services. They even did shopping and provided financial counseling. These women served fifteen months, "giving the longest period of active service of any of the colored women who went overseas."[26]

On the home front, the fifty thousand-member National Association of Colored Women, along with black female church groups and community service oriented auxiliaries, showed their collective patriotic fervor by waging their own campaigns to care for black service members assigned to segregated military camps.[27] Throughout World War I, representatives from these groups worked feverishly to build and buoy black troop morale, providing well-stocked care packages and hosting dinners and social events in their honor. Taking their support one step further, these African American female groups endeavored to make sure families were taken care of financially, properly fed and secure in their homes while the soldiers went off to war.

These groups in turn coordinated efforts with the Circle for Negro War Relief, Inc., an interracial group of influential upper-class men and women, to maximize their ability to provide aid and comfort to black troops. Featuring such executive members as W.E.B. Dubois and James Weldon Johnson, the Circle quickly became a highly structured organization. They provided leadership designed to determine the short- and long-term logistical and financial needs of deployed African American soldiers and their families and effectively tap resources of black churches and schools to meet those needs. By the war's end, the Circle's membership boasted fifty units in twenty-five states.[28] This type of well-coordinated collective support proved crucial in keeping the patriotic embers burning in the national black press and among the "empowering the Negro race" ideologues. Many of the latter had owned grave doubts about the wisdom of coaxing young black men to serve in a Jim Crow policy driven military.

Unfortunately, "the war to end all wars" did not end the war of racial discrimination against African American women, but it did give them more incentive to continue waging their own personal and collective battles and ultimately win the right to serve in their nation's military.

FLAGS OF THE NUBIAN SISTERS: AFRICAN AMERICAN WOMEN IN WORLD WAR II

World War II was a monumental moment for women. Although the age-old debate regarding women's fitness to serve in the military still raged in some social and professional circles, there was a growing realization that women had to serve in this war. From the onset of the war, President Franklin Roosevelt also faced tremendous pressure from the African American press. Patrick Washburn, noting the formidable influence of the black press, credited it with mounting a successful campaign for black military service.[29] Civil rights activist Dr. Mary McLeod Bethune also was instrumental in waging a relentless hands-on campaign to get African American women to serve. Bethune, president and founder of the National Council of Negro Women, was known to national politicians as an advocate for minorities and the oppressed. The presidential administrations of Coolidge and Hoover had appointed her to government positions. She was especially close to Franklin Roosevelt and his wife, Eleanor and became Roosevelt's special advisor on minority affairs. With Mrs. Roosevelt's assistance, Bethune successfully used this position as a powerful political platform to persuade the president to allow black women to serve in the military. Roosevelt finally capitulated to the collective pressure tactics of the African American leadership, media, and community, but it was still an uphill battle for African American women to gain entry into the military.

Not all black women who wanted to sign up for the military during World War II were able to do so. Rumors abound that some African American women, desperate to serve and able to pass for white, hid their race. A very restrictive service quota (10 % of the African American population at the time) meant that few would actually serve. To become a part of that 10 percent, black women had to take an aptitude test. Many prospective servicewomen failed the test, making them ineligible.[30]

Testing did not deter scores of African American women from attempting to sign up for the opportunity to serve their country. The Women's Army Auxiliary Corps was founded in 1942; it was renamed the Women's Army Corps in 1943. That year, forty African American women, dubbed the "ten percenters," went to Fort Des Moines, Iowa, for their initial WAAC officer training. As part of Dr. Bethune's strategic plan to propel African American women into military service leadership, she and other prominent black leaders carefully handpicked and screened the applicants. Failure would not be an option for these African American women of the first WAAC officer candidate class.

These women and the others who later joined them in Fort Des Moines over the next three years quickly learned that their training would take place in a pressure-laden media fish bowl. They were constantly watched, evaluated, and probed for any physical, mental, or moral weakness that would discredit their race. Skeptical segments of the American public vehemently opposed their service.

In 1942, Charity Adams became the first black WAAC commissioned officer. Over the next three years at Fort Des Moines, Adams built a national reputation as an expert supervisor, trainer, and commander of African

American female Army troops. In her autobiography, *One Woman's Army: A Black Officer Remembers the WAC,* Adams told how she constantly had to battle racist and sexist military superiors, colleagues, and subordinates who sought to derail her quest to be a good officer. After being promoted in rank and successfully advancing through a variety of challenging military job assignments at Fort Des Moines, Adams became the standard-bearer for exemplary African America servicewoman leadership.[31]

In March 1945, Major Adams, now a member of the Women's Army Corps, assumed command of the 6888th Central Postal Directory Battalion, an all-African American female unit responsible for ensuring the continuous delivery of mail to American troops in Europe. First assigned to Birmingham, England, the 832 enlisted women and thirty-one officers in the 6888th (nicknamed the six triple eight) quickly began to work in three eight-hour shifts, nonstop, seven days a week to clear 7 million pieces of backlogged items. There were three military aircraft hangars worth of letters and parcels. Given six months to complete a seemingly impossible task, they cleared it up in three months because they knew moving the mail was key to keeping the 7 million troops they served happy. Receiving mail was the ultimate morale booster, according to WAC Private Gladys O. Thompson: "Mail was important to the GIs because it was something that came from home. It was a way they could find out what was going on. It was personal and raised their spirits"[32] Six months after their initial assignment in England, the unit went to Paris to do the same type of mail sorting job. The 6888th was the only unit of African American women sent to serve in Europe.

Mission successfully accomplished, Adams left the service in March of 1946 as a lieutenant colonel, the highest-ranking black female officer in the WACS. In all, 6,520 African American women served as WAACS or WACS.

African American nurses once again fought for their right to join the military. Outlining their struggle, Carnegie noted that the initial Army Nurses Corps service member quota for black nurses was Fifty-six. Refusing appeasement, civil rights organizations and the African American press launched a vigorous protest against service quotas. The Army gradually removed the quotas and in 1943, allowed 160 to join. That year, the first group of black nurses to serve in this war on foreign soil went to Monrovia, Liberia, Africa. By the fall of 1944, 250 black women were in the ANC. Finally, by July 1945, with all racial restrictions lifted, there were 500 African American women nurses.[33]

Their service to the country was not without its problems with racism and sexism. In her autobiography, *The Challenge,* Margaret Bailey, the first black nurse promoted to colonel in the ANC, recounts a humiliating encounter she and other black nurses were briefly forced to endure in 1944 while serving at a German prisoner of war camp in Florence, Arizona. The African American nurses worked with white doctors and nurses but lived in segregated quarters. Their eating arrangements were also semi-segregated. All of the hospital personnel ate in the same dining hall, seated according to race and rank. Apparently fearing fraternization among the ranks, the black and white officers were moved to another eating area. The separation did not stop there. Bailey notes:

> As we black nurses arrived for lunch on the day of the change, a German prisoner of war standing at the door directed us to a room designated for us. "I said to him, Why not the room on the right? He replied, "You can't go into that room." All of the black nurses refused to go into our designated room. We went to our quarters feeling very sad. It was truly humiliating being directed to a segregated area by a German prisoner of war.[34]

The African American nurses refused to comply with the segregated eating facility order, and their white chief nurse refused to order them to comply unless the commanding officer put the order in writing. A stalemate ensued as some white doctors decided to further defy the edict and eat with the African American nurses. Media coverage of the incident, featured in a prominent African American newspaper, the *Pittsburgh Courier,* expedited the permanent rescinsion of this policy.

The Navy offered far more opposition to admitting African American women into its ranks. Once again, pressure from the black community had to be used to change the Navy's "no black women will serve" position. The first two African American female officers, Harriet Pickens and Frances Willis, received their commissions three days before Christmas, 1944.

Two months earlier, the Coast Guard had opened its doors to blacks, with only a handful of women actually enlisting in its female auxiliary. In October 1944, Yeoman Second Class Olivia J. Hooker was the first black woman to enlist in the Coast Guard. In January 1945, a few months before the war ended, four African American women finally served as Navy nurses. No African American women served in the Marines in any capacity. In 1949, the Marines became the last military service to allow black women to serve as nurses.[35]

While the Tuskegee Airman made a name for themselves in the skies for combat bravery and valor during World War II, two African American women were instrumental in getting black men into these coveted cockpits—Janet Harmon Bragg and Willa Brown. As outlined in her autobiography, *Soaring Above Setbacks,* from her youngest days, Bragg felt that even the sky should not be a limit. If birds could fly, why couldn't she? "As children, my brother Pat and I had watched birds fly, flaring their wing and tail feathers on alighting a branch or on the ground, where we would feed them crumbs. We noticed the way they always seemed to come in against the wind, just as with an airplane."[36]

In 1933, she began to take private flying lessons and even bought an airplane, but that was not enough. Determined to get her own commercial pilots license, she quickly signed up for lessons at the Aeronautical School of Engineering in Chicago, along with twenty-seven other African American men and women. Two African American licensed pilots, Cornelius Coffey and John Robinson, served as the flight instructors. According to Harmon-Bragg, these lessons were grueling. Students were required to learn how to fuel aircraft, prepare every mechanical structure of a plane, develop complex flight plans, and train for all types of emergency procedures. There were six women in her class. By the time, the demanding program ended, only Harmon Bragg and Willa Brown remained.

Both women worked hard to establish themselves in the aeronautical arena, but it was not easy for either. Willa Brown received her pilot's commercial license in 1937. Through an organization founded by Coffey, Brown, Robinson, and Bragg, the National Airmen's Association of America (NAAA), both women lobbied intensely for the inclusion of African Americans in the Civilian Pilot Training Program and the Army Air Corps. In 1939, NAAA eventually achieved success in their lobbying by getting the support and solid backing of Missouri Senator Harry S. Truman and first lady Eleanor Roosevelt. Just a year earlier, Harmon Bragg, Brown, who was now married to Coffey, and other black aviators had started their own airport in Robbins Illinois. They established the Coffee School of Aeronautics, which trained two hundred African American pilots over seven-years. Some of their pilot trainees went to Tuskegee Institute for further training and became members of the 99th Fighter Squadron, the Tuskegee airmen. In 1942, Willa Brown became the first African American officer in the Illinois wing of the Civil Air Patrol.

The NAAA victory did little to help grant Harmon Bragg the opportunity to fly for her country in World War II. First, the Women's Auxiliary Service Pilots program tried to discourage her from applying for WASP training because classes would be in Sweetwater, Texas. Undeterred, Harmon still insisted on having a chance to join the program and serve her country. The local coordinator, not wanting to be the bearer of bad news, passed the final decision on her application up the chain to the WASP national program director, Jacqueline Cochran. Cochran was a celebrated female pilot who had successfully lobbied the military and the government to get women into wartime cockpits. Harmon bitterly describes the aftermath of Cochran's decision:

> Finally she passed the buck, saying she would have to refer my case to Jacqueline Cochran at "headquarters." Eventually I received a telegram from Miss Cochran stating that "whatever Miss Sheehy told you still stands." In other words, I was refused because of the color of my skin. After this rejection, I

was upset, I knew I could fly. I even had my own plane! But this was a defeat, and something I could not accept.[37]

In an even more cruel twist of fate, Harmon Bragg could not even use her nurse's training in the Army's Nursing Corps. Another aspiring African American female aviator, Mildred Hemmons-Carter, received her pilot's wings in 1941 from Tuskegee Institute's Civilian Pilot Training Program, but she also was denied the right to become a WASP. Until the end of this war, the biggest battles most African American women who wanted to serve in the military fought were against racism and sexism.

OPERATION INTEGRATION: AFRICAN AMERICAN WOMEN'S SERVICE IN KOREA AND VIETNAM

In 1948, Congress passed the Women's Armed Services Integration Act, which allowed permanent service status in the regular armed forces to all women who were not in the nursing field. However, this act heavily restricted their service. Women could constitute only 2 percent of the total armed forces. They could not serve on naval vessels unless the ships were transports or hospital ships, and they had limited command opportunities. Female officers could not make up more than 10 percent of the 2 percent. The highest rank they could hope to attain was lieutenant colonel. There were also physical and age restrictions. Pregnant women had to leave the service, married or unmarried. Women had to retire prior to reaching menopause.

On July 26, 1948, one month after the passage of this act, President Harry S. Truman desegregated all of the armed forces, with Executive Order 9981. It was specifically designed to ban racial discrimination and segregation from the armed forces. In 1949, the Marines became the last military service to allow black women to serve, but the branch became the first to formally integrate. In 1950, the Navy allowed twenty-five black women to enlist. The Air Force, (formerly the Army Air Corps) integrated in 1949, and the Army in 1950. African American women nurses served during the Korean War alongside white nurses and colors in the MASH (Mobile Army Surgical Hospital) units and field hospitals.[38] Other African American women volunteered to serve in Army supply units and as administrative assistants in military bases in Japan, Okinawa, and the Philippines.[39] In 1951, Edwina Martin, Fannie Jean Cotton, and Evelyn Brown became the first three African American women to be graduated from the Air Force Officer Candidate School and commissioned.

Seventy-five African American women served in Vietnam. While some served as administrative assistants and supply personnel, some nurses in the Air Force and Army served under dangerous conditions while helping wounded U.S. troops. In 1967, retired ANC Colonel Marie Rodgers ran the operating room of the 24th Evacuation Hospital at Long Binh, South Vietnam, for six months. During that year, the unit treated 9,010 patients. About a third of those were treated and sent back to active duty. Rogers received the Bronze Star from President Johnson.[40] Captain Diane Lindsay, also in the ANC, was the first African American nurse to receive the Soldier's Medal for Heroism. In 1970, Colonel Clotilde Bowen, the first black woman physician to hold an Army commission, served in Vietnam as the Army's chief psychiatrist. Her duties included supervising seventeen other physician and nurse psychiatrists and social workers, as well as organizing and maintaining the Army's Vietnam drug and race relations programs. Marcelite Harris achieved a series of firsts during her career, which began when she served in Vietnam. In 1971, she became the first female aircraft maintenance officer, serving with the 49th Tactical Fighter Squadron in Korat, Thai Air Base, Thailand. In 1978, she became the first of two women to serve in command at the United States Air Force Academy. In 1986, she became the first woman deputy commander of maintenance. Harris was also the first African American woman to be promoted to major general.

In 1967, the Women's Services Integration Act was modified by Public Law 90-130 to eliminate the 2 percent cap on the number of enlisted and commissioned women who could serve. Women also became eligible to be promoted to general officer rank and were allowed to enlist in the National Guard.[41]

In 1973, the inception of the all-volunteer force allowed women the opportunity to serve in a wider capacity. Women also received a wider range of job assignments and more opportunities for promotion.

A year earlier, in 1972, Mildred C. Kelly became the first black female Army sergeant major, the highest Army enlisted rank. In 1975, Donna Davis became the first African American female Naval Medical Corp doctor. In 1979, Hazel Johnson scored two historical firsts by becoming the first black female general officer in the Department of Defense and the first black ANC chief. By the time she retired in 1983, after twenty-eight years of service, she had also become a doctor in her own right, receiving a Ph.D. in education from Catholic University of America In Washington, D.C.

In the 1970s, women entered the military academies and Army and Air Force ROTC programs. They became military pilots who fly certain types of aircraft (helicopters, transports, and carriers) and serve on certain types of ships. Women also became engineers, and military police personnel. African American Alice Henderson broke the religious gender barrier to become the first Armed Forces female chaplain.

In 1980, the DOPMA (Defense Officer Manpower Personnel Management Act) enabled women to serve equally in the same service status as men, eliminating the need for WAVES, WAFS, and WACS. That year, more than 170,000 women were serving as 8.5 percent of the U.S. Armed Forces.

African American women continued to thrive in active duty military service. One decade later, when almost 41,000 women deployed in support of Desert Storm, 40 percent were African Americans. Several were injured and three died in this conflict. African American women in the first Persian Gulf War were able to see and experience combat, like Army First Lieutenant Phoebe Jeter, who commanded an all-male Patriot missile unit that launched thirteen missiles and successfully shot down two enemy SCUD missiles. She was the only military service woman in command to do so. Others performed a variety of duties and endured the same stark desert combat conditions as their male counterparts (e.g., lack of clean shower facilities and latrines and inadequate sleeping facilities), performing many of the same duties. Thanks to extensive around-the-clock media coverage, Americans and the rest of the world were able to see just how well they handled combat. In later years Americans would also see how African American women continued to excel in leadership.

Michelle Howard took command of the USS Rushmore on March 12, 1999, becoming the first African American woman to command a ship in the U.S. Navy. When the twentieth century ended, because of the success of their Desert Storm service, African American women could serve in almost any type of military occupation, with the exception of Army infantry and Special Forces and Navy SEALS units. This important policy change allowed more women to serve in combat zones. There was an increase from 7 percent to nearly 24 percent among those who have served since 1990.

WINNING THE BATTLE TO FLY AND FIGHT: BLACK FEMALE AVIATORS SLIP THE SURLY BONDS OF RACISM

After World War II, it took over three decades for the Department of Defense to grant African American women the right to become fully recognized military aviators for their country. In 1979, Army 2nd Lieutenant Marcella A. Hayes became the first African American female pilot in the Armed Forces. The following year, Brenda Robinson became the first black naval female pilot assigned to the Fleet Logistics Squadron Forty in Norfolk, Virginia. In 1999, Air Force Academy graduate and Civil Air Patrol aviator Shawna Kimbrell became the service's first black female F-16 fighter pilot. She flew sorties to enforce a no fly zone over Iraq during Operation Northern Watch in 2001. In 2000, Christina Hopper, another African American female also became an F-16 pilot. While assigned to Cannon Air Force Base, New Mexico, her first duty station, she flew protection missions for the country in the immediate aftermath of the September 11, 2001, terrorist attacks. Later that year she deployed with her squadron to Kuwait as part of the 332nd Air Expeditionary Wing. She was the first black female Air Force pilot to fly over fifty combat and combat support missions in support of operations Southern Watch and Iraqi Freedom. Vernice Armour, as a 9H-W Super Cobra attack helicopter aviator became the first African American female United States Marine pilot. Serving two tours in Operation Iraqi Freedom in 2003 and 2004, she became the first African American female aviator in any of the services to see combat.

Merryl Tengesdal began her military aviator journey in the Navy in 1994 and for the next ten years served as an SH-60B Sea Hawk helicopter pilot. A decade later, she ascended further by switching military services and becoming the First African American woman to fly the Air Force's U-2 reconnaissance plane. Tengesdal has flown the U2 in intelligence gathering missions for operations Enduring Freedom and Iraqi Freedom.

In 2005, HC 130 aircraft pilot Jeanne McIntosh Menze became the first African American female pilot in the United States Coast Guard. According to Menze, her greatest challenge did not take place in the air but in the water; she had to learn how to swim in order to make it through the rigors of the Coast Guard's Water Survival Training. In 2010, La'Shanda Holmes became the first African American female helicopter pilot in the Coast Guard.

The top 1 percent of the enlisted rank of all of the services hold the coveted pay grade rank of E-9. Black women of all of the services have held this rank to distinction in war and peace time. A notable example is Army Command Sgt. Major Evelyn Hollin, who received a Bronze Star during Enduring Freedom and Iraqi Freedom in 2004. She became the first African American woman to head a combat arms unit when she assumed command of the 1st Battalion, 31st Air Defense Artillery. Teresa King, also a Command Sergeant Major, became the first female commandant of the Army's Drill Sergeant School in 2009.

At this writing, the number of African American servicewomen is at its highest level. Undoubtedly there will be more significant history to record that captures the exploits of dedicated individuals. As retired Colonel Lorry M. Fenner, who has studied the history of women in the military, noted:

> Marginalized groups must also have an accessible history and public memory of their contribution to make advances and to play a part in constructive change. Minority groups including Blacks, women and homosexuals, have been denied their history/memory as well as their voices. Retrieving these voices is essential to their struggle against inequality and exclusion. If they are denied their history, as women have been, they cannot use it in support of current debates on their service.[42]

NOTES

1. Catherine Clinton, *The Black Soldier: 1492 to the Present* (Boston: Houghton Mifflin, 2000).

2. Debra Newman, "Black Women in the Era of the American Revolution in Pennsylvania," *Journal of Negro History* 61.3 (July 1976): 276–289.

3. Gail Lumet Buckley, American Patriots: The Story of Blacks in the Military from the Revolution to Desert Storm (New York: Random House, 2000), xvii.

4. Ibid. Rudolph Alexander, *Racism, African Americans and Social Justice* (Lanham, MD: Rowman and Littlefield, 2005), 70–71.

5. Alexander, *Racism, African Americans and Social Justice.* Darlene Clark Hine, ed., *Black Women in America*, 2d ed., "Revolutionary War." (New York: Oxford University Press, 2005).

6. Hine, *Black Women in America.*

7. Buckley, *American Patriots.*

8. Lerone Bennett Jr., *Before the Mayflower: A History of Black America* (New York: Penguin, 1989), p. 207.

9. Accessed at www.harriettubman.com/pension.html.

10. Susie King Taylor, *Reminiscences of My Life in Camp with the 33d United States Colored Troops Late 1st S. C. Volunteers* (Boston: self published, 1902; repr. ed., New York: Markus Weiner, 1988), 35.

11. Ibid., 31–32.

12. Ibid., 21.

13. M. Elizabeth Carnegie, The Path We Tread: Blacks in Nursing Worldwide, 1854–1994, 3d ed. (Sudbury, MA: Jones & Bartlett, 1995). Lisa King, "In Search of Women of African Descent Who Served in the Civil War Union Navy," The Journal of Negro History 83.4 (1998): 302–311. Jane Schultz, "Seldom Thanked, Never Praised and Scarcely Recognized: Gender and Racism in Civil War Hospitals," Civil War History 48. 3 (September 2002): 220–235.

14. Schultz, "Seldom Thanked," 221–22.

15. King, "In Search."

16. Taylor, *Reminiscences*, 67–68.

17. Frank N. Schubert, *Voices of the Buffalo Soldiers: Records, Reports and Recollections of Military Life and Service in the West* (Albuquerque: University of New Mexico Press, 2003).

18. Ibid.

19. Ibid.

20. Brenda L. Moore, *To Serve My Country, to Serve My Race. The Story of the Only African American WACS Stationed Overseas During World War II* (New York: New York University Press, 1996), 116.

21. Carnegie, *The Path We Tread.*

22. Kathryn Sheldon, "Brief History of Black Women in the Military," Web site, Women in Military Service for America Memorial Foundation, 2007. Accessed at http://www.womensmemorial.org/Education/BBH1998.html.

23. Carl Schneider and Dorothy Schneider, "American Women in World War I," *Social Education,* 58.2 (February 1994): 83–85.

24. Addie W. Hunton and Kathryn M. Johnson, *Two Colored Women with the Expeditionary Force*, (Brooklyn, NY: Brooklyn Eagle Press, 1920).

25. Ibid., 23.

26. Ibid., 39.

27. Nikki Brown, Private Politics and Public Voices : Black Women's Activism from World War I to the New Deal (Bloomington, IN: Indiana University Press, 2006).

28. Ibid., 39.

29. Patrick S. Washburn, The African American Newspaper: Voice of Freedom, Medill Visions of the American Press Series (Evanston, IL: Northwestern University Press, 2006).

30. Brenda L. Moore, "African-American women in the U.S. military," Armed Forces & Society 17 (spring 1991): 363–384.

31. Charity Earley Adams, *One Woman's Army: A Black Officer Remembers the WAC.* Texas A&M University Military History Series, #12, 2d ed. (College Station, TX: Texas A&M University Press, 1996).

32. Quoted in Yvonne Latty, *We Were There: Voices of Africans American Veterans from World War II to the War in Iraq* (New York: Harper Collins, 2004), 36.

33. Carnegie, *The Path We Tread*, 174–179

34. Margaret E. Bailey, *The Challenge: Autobiography of Colonel Margaret E. Bailey* (Chicago: Tucker, 1999), 29–30.

35. Carnegie, *The Path We Tread*.

36. Janet Harmon Bragg and Marjorie M. Kriz, Soaring Above Setbacks: The Autobiography of Janet Harmon Bragg, Smithsonian History of Aviation and Spaceflight Series (Washington: Smithsonian Institution Press, 1996), 26.

37. Ibid., 40.

38. Loring Manning, *Women in the Military: Where They Stand*, 5th ed. (Washington: Women's Research and Education Institute, 2005), 2.

39. Judith Bellafaire, "Volunteering for Risk: Black Military Women Overseas During the Wars in Korea and Vietnam." Website, Women in Military Service Memorial Foundation, Inc. Accessed at 199.236.85.13/Education/BWOHistory.html.

40. Latty, *We Were There*, 128.

41. Manning, *Women in the Military*.

42. Lorry Fenner 1996, 23.

Chapter Three

"Sistahs" of Defense

Duties and Dangers of African American Women in Service in the Gulf Wars

We were living in tents. In the buildings where the officers lived you could still see the bullet holes in the walls from the massacre.
—Maria Quillan, Navy E-5, Operation Iraqi Freedom

My uncle told me to keep my head close to the ground and not to try to be a hero.
—Courtney Salter, Army specialist, Operation Iraqi Freedom

So tell me, exactly where is the safety in "noncombat jobs during war? There is none. It's war! So if we are dying, losing limbs, and becoming prisoners like men, why are women being kept out of combat roles?
—Shoshana Johnson, Army specialist, Operation Iraqi Freedom

The stark reality that the manifold dangers and ravages of war could strike close to home when least expected came after my beeper went off while I was sitting in church on February 1, 1991. As soon as I got to a telephone I made a quick call and received terse instructions from a military officer. I was to return to my military base immediately. During a tense fifteen-minute drive to the base I wondered what could have happened.

For eight months, over half of the active duty forces of Eaker Air Force Base, Arkansas' 97th Bombardment Wing, had been deployed through Europe and the Persian Gulf Theater as part of a massive coalition force buildup in operations Desert Shield/Storm. Based on the cryptic tone of my telephone summons I worried that one of our B52H large strategic bombers or KC135 refueling and cargo carrying aircraft might have crashed or been shot down

41

by Iraqi forces. These planes were temporarily deployed to military bases on the island of Diego Garcia and near Bentwaters, England.

When I arrived at Eaker's Command Post, the base's nerve center for war operations, I discovered that my worst fears were true. One of our deployed B 52Hs had crashed while returning from a daylight weapons release mission in support of Operation Desert Storm. Wreckage was scattered over the Indian Ocean, fifteen miles off Diego Garcia and the U.S. Navy base where coalition forces were launching air operations. More alarming, four of the six crew members had ejected from the aircraft. Three were miraculously rescued from the ocean as they floated dangerously close to burning fuel and the aircraft fuselage. A day later, another crew member's lifeless body was found floating in a raft. Two crew members' bodies were never found. That B52H from Eaker was the only aircraft of its kind lost during Operation Desert Storm.

The news hit hard on the base and in the nearby small town of Blytheville.[1] There was little time for me to grieve. As the base's public affairs officer, I had to immediately launch a comprehensive media plan that would govern how we handled endless queries from international, national, regional and local media.

Over the next two days my three person staff and I handled more than 200 media queries. Regional media called from Memphis, Tennessee. National and international media organizations were particularly ruthless and relentless in their pursuit of "the war story." To counter their over-exuberance before it made sensationalized coverage, we trained volunteers to answer media questions and protect the crewmembers' families from being overwhelmed. Reporters and TV camera crews even tried to enter a local elementary school to track down the children of one of the air crew members. A brash media television crew tried to attend a church service to interview one of the wives.

In all fairness, I understood the motivation behind their frenetic chasing after such a journalistic scoop. Any story of a military plane crash in peacetime or war is compelling in a macabre way. The death of three crew members made this particular military plane crash an even more salacious media bonanza. There was the fairy tale turned tragic loss of a newlywed crewmember who had married just two weeks before deploying. His very young, shell shocked widow sometimes descended into wild sobbing jags, punctuated by angry profanity laced rants about an uncaring military system that had left her without even a body to bury. All of these elements made for great prime time news.

Two days later, when it was finally time to grieve, the Eaker family did so in solidarity, packing the small base chapel to capacity. When the senior chaplain opened the somber memorial service by gently intoning the words of Isaiah 40:1, "Comfort ye, Comfort ye my people, saith your God," pent up emotions that had been held in icy military check began to slowly melt into a cathartic pool of collective mourning. The service moved through heartfelt renderings of poignant tributes to the three fallen aircrew officers, and stoic scripture readings paying homage to military victory and service. The solemn singing of spiritual anthems extolling righteousness and life's noble sacrifices in battle, elicited muffled sobs. I could not help but look around the crowded chapel and see the tear streaked faces of the spouses of those still deployed in support of this war, especially those married to B52 and KC 135 air crew members.

When the service ended, military and civilian people of all ranks lined up quietly to give hugs and offer whispered words of encouragement to those family members left behind and especially to the heavily sedated newlywed widow. I passed a group of B52 aircrew wives, huddled together in a group. Some were rocking back and forth, and some wept less silently than before. I could see fear and uncertainty on their faces as they wondered, "Will my husband come home safely, and when?" In March 1991, the rest of the 97th BMW B52 and KC135 aircrews and all of the other Eaker personnel who had deployed in support of operations Desert Shield/Storm returned home safely to great celebration and fanfare.

The loss of that big bomber plane would always remind me that the dangers of war can strike any time and irrevocably change and maim the lives of those who serve and of the families and friends who enable them to do so.

"WE'RE REALLY AT WAR!" AFRICAN AMERICAN WOMEN IN DESERT SHIELD/STORM

When President George W. Bush called for a cease fire in February 1991, most of the American troops who had deployed in 1990 for Operation Desert Shield or at the outset of Operation Desert Storm in January 1991 began to come home. Those who came back were replaced by other troops from all branches of the services. Despite the cease fire, there was still a combat zone in the Gulf. Coalition forces had established a no fly zone to deter Saddam Hussein from reneging on the cease fire and starting more trouble with Kuwait and neighboring Saudi Arabia.

That August I volunteered to go to Riyadh, Saudi Arabia, but was quickly transferred to the United States Central Command Air Forces (CENTAF Forward) headquarters Dhahran, Saudi Arabia, because of "cultural and gender sensitivities." Before I had even left the United States, then Brigadier General Eugene D. Santarelli, who was to be my boss during my time in the desert, decided that my being female would hinder my effectiveness as an Air Force public affairs/protocol officer.[2] The reason is that I would be working with Saudi military forces and the ultra-conservative mutaween, Saudi government appointed religious police, in the Saudi Arabian capital.

I began my seven day a week twelve-hour shifts upon arrival in Dhahran. I had only been there a few weeks when an Air Force fighter jet assigned to the 4404th (Provisional) Wing crashed while enforcing the no fly zone. The pilot safely ejected. A routine military aircraft crash board investigation determined that a part had malfunctioned. I worked with a representative of the U.S. Central Command public affairs Air Force department to gather approved information for national and international media and quickly dispel rumors that the aircraft had been shot down. Emboldened by the fact that one of their enemy's aircraft had shown itself to be vulnerable, a few brave Iraqi pilots spent more time fine tuning their "aerial chicken games." They pushed the rules of engagement envelope by flying as close to the no fly zone as possible.

My public affairs duties were seemingly mundane compared to the responsibilities of those who had been there for the actual combat. My small staff published a daily newspaper for Army and Air Force troops and photographed soldiers at work in their daily combat duties. I dealt with the usual multi-level military bureaucracy when coordinating media query answers and requests for interviews with the local U.S. Central Command (USCENT-COM) public affairs officials.[3] As the CENTAF protocol officer, I also worked with the Army Protocol and Public Affairs divisions as the Air Force's event planner. I helped coordinate how and when senior U.S. and Saudi military officers came together to meet and socialize.

During my time in Dhahran, I was always aware that that I was in a combat zone. Danger could break out at any moment, despite the formal cease fire and no fly zone enforcement. As part of my disaster preparedness training, I had learned how to use and fire a .38 caliber and a 9 mm handgun. As an officer I had the choice of opting out of M16 rifle training, which I did. During mock disaster exercises I wore chemical protective body gear in the workplace. I even learned how to properly seal a gas mask while stating my name and social security number in a chamber filled with gas. Before I deployed for Desert Storm, I became reacquainted with these skills, skills that could save my life in a real combat zone. While I frequently contemplated the possibility of danger, I was not afraid, nor were those around me. To discover what made men and women stand stalwart in the face of adversity, I began listening to the stories of those from all of the Armed Forces who, like me, had become part of a unique combat experience that few would ever forget. Years later, these stories stayed with me and now when it comes to African American women military service in the gulf I am finally begin to tell them.

"SISTAHS" OF DEFENSE: AFRICAN AMERICAN WOMEN COME FACE TO FACE WITH COMBAT

As stated earlier, most African American women did not initially envision going into combat at any time during their military service. They were drawn to the military for many reasons. For some, military service was a family tradition. Others relished being able to travel and live all over the world at the government's expense. Others wanted to take advantage of attaining advanced academic degrees and relying on the security of steady employment. Black women especially appreciated the opportunity to become managers and leaders in a variety of career fields quicker and more frequently than their civilian counterparts.

For those who signed up for military service with such reasoning, combat was the furthest thing from their minds. Since the Revolutionary War, the country's patriarchal infrastructure allowed the executive and legislative branches of the government to ban women from participating in combat-related jobs and being directly assigned to units fighting in declared combat zones. However, prior to operations Desert Shield and Desert Storm, small groups of women had already begun blurring combat lines by participating in military skirmishes. This was true in Operation Urgent Fury in 1983, when the United States invaded Grenada to save medical students, and in Operation Just Cause, the 1989 invasion of Panama to depose General Manuel Noriega. When operations Desert Shield/Storm came, combat lines would stay blurred, gender wise, into the twenty-first century.

Coreen Reyes, who during ten-years as an Army officer was a combat arms adjutant, an assignments officer, and eventually a company commander, helped blur that line. She was a 1986 Hampton (Virginia) University Army ROTC graduate. In 1990 she was part of 1st Armored Division Support Command, a first lieutenant in the 400th Personnel Services Company. As the company's executive officer she wrote military plans, got weapons supplies, and did all of the paperwork to help her unit and others prepare to deploy for war.

Before receiving word through official military channels, she learned from a CNN newscast that her unit was deploying. They went to Europe first and then to Tent City, Riyadh, Saudi Arabia, where she remained while she was in the Gulf region. She quickly became a leader in her own right but found out that leadership was not always glamorous. "I was there for one month in the most miserable of conditions. We had to dig foxholes. At five feet, three and one-half inches I had to dig latrines large enough for the tallest person in the unit to use, our commander, who was six foot, three inches tall." She also ended up having to do more than her fair share of digging because her commander had "shoulder problems." Nor did he appreciate her willingness to set a good leadership example for their troops. At every opportunity her captain would berate her and even questioned Coreen's ability to lead in front of everyone. He constantly criticized her and their troops for the smallest mistakes, real or imagined. It seemed that he was trying to set her up for a fall, undermining her authority and openly disparaging her sense of command. These potentially dangerous personality clashes between the two could have given him ammunition to stop her from advancing as an officer.

But fate has a way of intervening at the most unexpected times. After a series of bizarre mishaps, the captain was relieved of his command. Lapses in personal judgment proved to be his undoing. He would often disappear and was noticeably absent every time his supervisors came to the encampment looking for him. When he returned after these strange absences, he would brag about taking a shower or making calls to his wife, things no one who worked for him was able to do. When he was "fired" from his job, Reyes became the company commander. She had been a captain for all of one week. As the newly appointed commander of 100 people, she, a junior company grade officer, filled a field grade officer's slot of major. Reyes was the only senior female servicewoman in her company.

To further inspire herself in her leadership style, she took to heart her training at Hampton University. ROTC mentors had told her, "You must be better. Set an example. Be the absolute best you can be. Treat everyone the way you would want to be treated." Her command leadership confidence thrived as she, in her words, "worked it like I did in the field. The paperwork went as smooth as silk. OERs (officers' evaluation reports) were being processed and promotion board met on time." She had no problems when providing briefings and reports to her senior officers. Outside of a few disciplinary challenges, none of her troops gave her serious problems. She treated them well and they rewarded her respect for them by "doing their job."

Reyes's stint as company commander was hard work, but it also had its amusing moments. Some of them had to do with the fact that she shared her tent with her sergeant major, an older, married white male and the highest ranking enlisted person under her command. Her berthing arrangements were a tad bit awkward, she noted, but the two of them worked things out.

Coreen never felt that she was in actual danger and says she did not think about danger, even though her husband was a pilot, flying Black Hawk helicopter combat missions into Iraq. She wasn't worried because she knew he was well trained and skilled. Whenever he could, her husband would catch a ride in a military vehicle to come to see her, providing small comfort and reassurance to both of them.

Looking back on her time as commander, Coreen offers advice for women who will lead in future military conflicts: "One must be genuine. Be yourself. They [the troops] also know if you are being fake. I had to be me because at the end of the day it's you in the mirror."

"WE BRAKE FOR CAMELS": A CHRONICLE OF COURAGEOUS CARGO MISSIONS

Gidgetti Greathouse found herself serving in the Army against her mother's wishes. Undaunted, after basic training at Fort Dix, New Jersey, she was sent to Germany and became a heavy vehicle truck driver. She initially assured her mother in 1989 that the United States would not go to war against anyone, but Gidgetti had to eat her words. In 1990 her unit deployed to the desert. Her commander said that the equipment would not go unless the people who drove them also went. Her family worried about her deploying so much that her brother offered to go to war in her place. His gesture was moot. She was going to deploy with her unit in support of Operation Desert Shield and help maintain the valuable military equipment.

During Desert Shield/Storm, driving became Gidgetti's outlet. She volunteered to go on as many driving missions as possible because she did not want to sit around and think about the fact that she really was in the midst of a war. "I racked up the most mileage in my unit," she said proudly. Still, danger was always on the horizon. The large trucks Gidgetti drove were slow and lumbering, easy targets for Iraqi missiles as well as land mines. She carried dangerous cargo, including artillery shells, rocket launchers, and other types of ammunition. She always was accompanied by a soldier armed with a shotgun because the enemy prized these large vehicles as targets. Sometimes she drove on roads littered with burning Iraqi vehicles, aircraft, and smoldering corpses.

During one mission, Gidgetti was driving on what became known as the "Highway of Death." "I drove through burning flesh and charred bodies. You could see the bodies actually on the roads. The smell was horrible. I had to concentrate on not looking around and listening to the cries." Her escort suddenly told her told her to drive and not look around, no matter what. Her curiosity ultimately overwhelmed her. She couldn't help but look around. Lodged in the grating at the rear of the truck was a disembodied arm. "I saw it and began freaking out."

Her escort had to slowly and carefully talk her through the process of driving through such a ghastly scene. "I want you to pull over. I need you to look the other way," he said carefully. First, he told her she could not allow herself to become personally involved. Like it or not, she had to be detached, focused solely on her mission's task. "He told me to . . . do what I need to do to get back home." Thinking of her family and her desire to see them again, she finally got herself together.

The most serious dangers she had to face when driving in the desert came from nature. If you broke down in an isolated section of the desert, there was no quick rescue, she noted. "They gave you an extra box of water and said, "We'll see you in a couple of days."

"We had to constantly brake for camels," she recalled. Sand blew into the truck's mechanical systems, and potholes were unavoidable. Trucks broke down frequently. "We were robbing Peter to pay Paul. We had to constantly cannibalize [borrow parts from one vehicle to repair another] to keep them operational." Scavenging parts from other vehicles was not always enough. Her truck partner, Sergeant Nixon, performed mechanical miracles when their trucks broke down. "He used all kinds of things to get them back up— tape, camera parts, milk cartons. That man could work magic. He got the trucks going really quick." Tires constantly exploded in the heat. At first these explosions scared her, but after a while, she became a "tire changing virtuoso."

Other mechanical mishaps became routine occurrences. Once, a trailer she was pulling caught on fire. She and her rifle carrying bodyguard had to detach the trailer and leave it in the desert. Their superiors eventually made them return to retrieve it.

It could be difficult to follow traveling directions. Once on a night convoy she found out that someone had given them errant directions that took the procession she was a part of into a land mined pit. Slowly and carefully everyone in the convoy walked out of that mined area "by the grace of God," she said. Incredibly, she added, the drivers and riders were ordered to go back into that field and drive the vehicles out. Gidgetti said no one could believe the insanity of the order. "They told us to back the vehicles out. We refused to do it, and they gave us letters of reprimand." The administrative punishment, which could ruin a career, was finally rescinded once her unit returned to the United States. Their battalion commander contended that there should have been sufficient military reconnaissance to avoid such a mistake.

Looking back on her time in Desert Storm, Gidgetti admits spending a lot of time crying and praying. Knowing that she could have been a target and gotten kidnapped or killed at any moment made her appreciate living even more.

MAIL, MAYHEM, AND MIRACLES: TEXANS WITHSTAND GULF WAR INCIDENTS

Patricia Johnson joined the Army right out of high school because she wanted to get out of Texas. After basic training, she was the only woman in her military police unit serving in Panama during the Just Cause conflict. A few years later, Johnson turned in her military police baton and badge and become a postal clerk specialist.

Arriving in Saudi Arabia in early January 1991, she immediately went to work building the camp's post office. Mail was stacked up. Since getting mail was a big morale booster, it became important for Patricia to do all she could to help get the packages and letters moving quickly. Following in the footsteps of the African American female 6668th Postal Directory Battalion in World War II, Patricia joined with other postal units in the area to help get backlogged mail out to troops. She and the postal unit workers had to work twenty-four hours a day, seven days a week, because of the sheer volume of mail. Handling mail in Saudi Arabia was complicated by Saudi laws banning certain items. Family members, at the request of some service member, would send forbidden items such as alcohol in their care packages. "We had to be on constant alert," she noted.

What little extra time she had was spent filling sandbags and constructing protective bunkers. She also helped put together a makeshift post exchange.

She was eating in the mess hall when a level-four danger alarm sounded. An Iraqi SCUD missile apparently had been launched in the direction of the camp. Immediate pandemonium ensued as people tried to put on their gas masks and other chemical protective gear. "Everyone panicked. It was total chaos," she said. Patricia and a younger female solider dove under a table. The young woman was screaming and sobbing. Patricia grabbed her hands and told her, "We gotta pray. We held hands and prayed until things had calmed down. That was the scariest time of my life."

Even walking guard duty could provide moments of fear. On a two-hour walk around the camp perimeter, a young female soldier from Louisiana who was on guard duty with Patricia began to panic. She became increasingly hysterical. "She was saying things like 'What if we get shot?' 'What if we get our throats cut?' I thought she was going to have a nervous breakdown. I felt so sorry for her," Patricia said. Wearing on Patricia's already severely frayed nerves, the young solider blubbered through the entire two hours.

Only Patricia's resolute faith and her desire to return home to see her family carried her through scary experiences during her deployment.

Another Texan, Felicia Weston, joined the Army in 1987. After finishing basic training at Fort Jackson, South Carolina, she went to Fort Gordon, Georgia, for Advanced Individual Training. Three years later she was a part of Signal Battalion Charley (C) Company, on the way to the Gulf. She ended up in Dhahran, Saudi Arabia, while the rest of her unit went to Riyadh, Saudi Arabia. It was hard to be separated from her unit, but she enjoyed her work. She provided communication support to a variety of units and spent a lot of time attaching and fixing telephones.

On February 25, 1991, she had returned to her room after twelve-hour shift. Suddenly the windows in her room exploded in her face. A SCUD missile had been fired from Iraq. Although journalistic and military accounts vary, fiery parts of the missile fell into the compound where Felicia lived. A large ammunition cache stored near the makeshift barracks exploded. Disoriented by the explosion, the smoke, and the noise, Felecia grabbed her gas mask. "I ran out of the door, and someone said, 'You're bleeding; you are bloody.'" Felicia ran on, determined to protect herself from the possible effects of chemical attack and to get away from the burning building that was starting to fall apart around her. "I tried to get my mask on. I tried to seal it but, because of the blood, it would not seal."

Still disoriented, she ran into the courtyard. There she was confronted by the aftermath of the explosion. All around her, people were wailing and running around in alarm. Saudi rescue crews from Dhahran and coalition rescue military units initially were thwarted from getting to the scene by hordes of curious Saudi neighborhood citizens who had been attracted to the gore of the scene. "They were videoing, taking pictures of the wounded and dead."

Meanwhile, blood was still pouring into her eyes and burning them. She could not see. Shards of glass were embedded all over her body. Temporarily blinded, she had no control over her situation. She had to entrust herself to others. Felicia was taken to a Mobile Army Surgical Hospital (MASH) unit. Her trip was pretty frightening. "There was a guy who kept screaming "I can't feel my legs. He had lots of injuries." During the ride, she could hear radio reports about deaths and injuries in the compound. "So many people had died. I just broke down and cried." Fortunately, two guardian angels in human form were riding with her. Two female Lieutenants stayed with her, constantly reassuring her. "They took care of me, told me everything was going to be okay."

Felicia received good care once she was in the hands of the medical personnel in the MASH unit. Three days later her commander from her original home unit came from Riyadh to visit and pray with her. Felicia was the only person from her home unit who had been injured. He took her back to their battalion in Riyadh, and she left Saudi Arabia with her unit. "If I had stayed in Dhahran, I would have been able to go back home earlier. The other unit in the camp with me went home after the explosion," she said.

The attack in which Felicia was injured ended up killing more people than did the seventy SCUD attacks on Israel and Saudi Arabia combined. Ninety-nine soldiers were wounded; twenty-nine of them fatally. Ironically the Iraqi missile was fired hours after Iraq said it would leave Kuwait.

After the long process of recovering from her wounds, she was sent back to Saudi Arabia in 1994 to work with a Patriot missile unit. "I put up a fight. I did not want to go back." There was, however, a shortage of signal personnel in her unit. The deployment attrition rate of troops from her signal company became more acute and desperate as women in her unit became pregnant and had to be sent home. Some who were stateside were not able to deploy because they also had become pregnant. Her first deployment in operations Desert Shield/Storm was for six months. Upon her return to Saudi Arabia, she served for eight months.

She was one of the fortunate ones who came through the SCUD attack, but she still suffers from survivor's guilt. Each day she thinks of those who didn't make it and wonders why she was spared. "I told God I would do whatever He wanted." Keeping that promise compelled her to visit veterans in VA hospitals who were wounded in battle physically, emotionally, and mentally, something she continues to do.

DODGING DANGER: AFRICAN AMERICAN WOMEN IN IRAQ

Air Force reservist, Major Gwendolyn Sheppard, a civil engineer officer from Wisconsin, deployed to Baghdad in July 2003 after her civil engineer squadron was formally activated that March. Gwendolyn was raised as a "military brat." She joined the Air Force National Guard in Missouri and then transferred to the California Air National Guard. She received a commission in the Navy Reserve and a direct commission with the Seabees in February 1989. In 1994, Navy Ensign Sheppard moved to Milwaukee. In 1997 she changed over to the Air Force Reserve and became Air Force Captain Sheppard.

As part of her academic preparation, she attended the Air Force Academy for two years and finished her engineering degree at North Carolina State University, Durham. During Operation Iraqi Freedom, her primary job was to plan and execute a wide range of construction projects to help with support missions. For example, her squadron worked on the upgrade for an aeromedical faculty, converting it from a thirty-bed to a fifty-bed shelter. To boost troop morale, she also worked on construction plans for a base food court, complete with a barbershop and flower shop.

As always in a combat area, there was an element of danger. While Gwendolyn did not participate in direct combat with the Iraqi forces, her unit and the coalition forces around her had a few close calls. She always slept with her Kevlar vest and gas mask nearby. At night a lights out policy for the base was strictly enforced. Troops had to sleep with their tent flaps tightly closed so that no light would seep through. Once, at 3:30 a.m., a rocket propelled grenade hit the runway. Immediately she and other members of the base responded. "I got up to make sure that all of my people were accounted for. Then for safety's sake we had to do a check of the perimeter the civil engineer unit was responsible for to make sure that there was no unexploded ordnance around." During another attack, a rocket grenade (RPG) hit a truck in the compound. A civil engineer fire truck put the fire out, she remembered.

Her unit was also responsible for maintaining a morgue. On July 22, 2003, Saddam Hussein's two oldest sons, Uday and Qusay, were brought there after being killed by U.S. Special Forces. While the Hussein brothers' bodies were in the morgue, the security around the base was extreme. Scores of high level U.S. and Iraqi officials came to the morgue to view the remains and aid in the task of positive identification.

All of the secrecy and around-the-clock security surrounding the morgue and its VIP contents took a toll on everyone, she said. "Having the Hussein brothers in the morgue was scary because we did not know what was going to happen." Base commanders feared that angry Iraqis loyal to Hussein would try to steal the bodies or that insurgents would launch a retaliatory attack. There was a collective sigh of relief when the bodies were taken from the morgue, she remembered.

Courtney Salter was almost deprived of achieving her dream of military service. She planned to enlist in the Air Force one year after she graduated from high school. An Air Force recruiter was extremely interested in signing her up until he found out that Courtney had a son. If you went into the military as a single parent, you would have to sign custody of your child over to a guardian. The Air Force recruiter refused to work with her any longer, but an Army recruiter stepped up to recruit her. When she pressed the recruiter about the child custody rule, the ethically challenged recruiter told her not to volunteer any information. When it came time to fill out the reams of paper work she had to sign to enter the military, the recruiter told her it would be better to omit the information about her son. As she got to basic training, others gave her the same advice. "Don't worry about it," they told her. When she was halfway through Advanced Individual Training, the omission caught up with her, and she was summoned before the judge advocate, the Army post legal counsel. The recruiter's advice to ignore military regulations was regarded as fraud. Fortunately, her case took a strange turn. "When I got to the judge advocate, they asked me if I wanted to stay in the Army. What direction did I want to go?" When she told them that she really wanted to be in the Army, she was released and nothing more was said about the custody issue. She became a supply specialist.

After the September 11, 2001, terrorist attack, military units around the country prepared to deploy. The sergeant major of the aviation brigade at Hunter Auxiliary Airfield, in Savannah, Georgia, told the troops to get ready. "He told us all to pack our bags. We were going to war."

The battalion sergeant major was just as blunt. "He told us to look to the left and right of us. The person who you are sitting next to might not be coming home. Everyone was afraid." Instilling fear in the young soldiers seemed to be the best thing the sergeant major felt he could do besides training and preparing them for war. "He told us that if we were not afraid, we needed to be. Even he was afraid."

For a year after 9/11, their training time in the field and on the firing range escalated. In November 2002, when the first actual call came for Courtney's unit to get ready to deploy, she was at Patrick AFB in Cocoa Beach, Florida, serving on a military funeral detail. When she came back she had an early Christmas with her son and prepared to leave. Her unit left January 26, 2003, and arrived in Kuwait January 27. This was her first airplane flight, and it was twenty-three hours long, complete with turbulence.

Landing in Kuwait at night she experienced complete culture shock. "There was nothing but dirt and tents." When they got to their large tents, there were not enough cots to go around. They also had to share their tent with fuel and ammunition units. The officers slept in their own tent. One female lieutenant, however, stayed with the enlisted women. "She was really nice," Courtney said. Some of the enlisted ended up having to sleep on the floor, but Courtney was so tired she did not care. Originally all of the enlisted women from the different units slept together on one side of the tent while men slept on the other side. The more senior enlisted women put up ponchos to form a curtain. Most women in her tent were African Americans.

The living dynamics in the tent changed when members of the fuel and ammo units got into a disagreement with the rest. The women in those units moved to the men's side. Courtney did not have time to worry about her sleeping arrangements. For the next month, she set up a mini operations center and supply area and a small post exchange. There also was more intensive training to get ready for their movement to Baghdad.

In early February, Courtney became part of a logistical advance team that left Kuwait two days before the rest of their unit. As a Humvee driver for an Army captain, she joined a convoy to Bagdad. In her Humvee was the captain, a warrant officer, and a first sergeant. She was the only female and the most junior ranked person in the vehicle. The convoy ride to Baghdad was long and fraught with problems and danger. Initially, Courtney was afraid because her driving skills were going to be tested in the field. "I had just started driving before I joined the Army," she admits. The driving conditions would have tested even the most expert of drivers. First, none of their equipment was in top condition. The natural elements also were hazardous. "There were dust-storms everywhere. I could not see anything in front of me."

Convoy speed limits were thirty miles per hour; at times Courtney had to go at least forty-five to keep up with the rest of the convoy. A Humvee's maximum speed was fifty. Courtney was determined to drive as fast as she could in order to keep up. "I told myself that I was not going to get lost. I was not going to be left behind: 'I may have an accident, but you are not going to leave me.'" Someone finally decided that slowing the convoy down was acceptable to keep the vehicles together. For the big vehicles, slowing down meant that they would get stuck in the soft sand. The larger vehicles were carrying ammunition for the helicopters, so they could not risk getting stranded.

As an added pressure, she had to make sure she was in line with everyone else and going in the right direction. Sometimes vehicles would pass her Humvee or cut in and out of the convoy line. Initially radio communication with those in the convoy was constant to ensure that each convoy member knew what direction to go, but the frequencies eventually became jammed, and they started losing contact.

While she was driving, she hit a manhole and everyone in the Humvee was bounced into the air. "They kept telling me to slow down and I told them, no, I would not slow down." The trip was hot, uncomfortable, and long. Everyone was becoming exhausted.

The objective was for the convoy to join the main advance body on the way to Baghdad. That did not happened right away. The original plan to travel with the main body began to unravel, as two of the larger vehicles did, in fact, get stuck in the sand. "We intended to meet up with the main body as they came up from the rear, but they detoured when they discovered that vehicles were getting stuck."

Courtney's captain decided that their Humvee and the other vehicles left in the convoy should follow his navigational instincts. He and the warrant officer, who was the only one in the Humvee who had actually deployed to the Gulf before, vehemently argued as to which way to go. Despite everyone's fears that the captain was leading them in the wrong direction, Courtney continued to drive as he ordered.

Fires appeared in the distance on her left and right. Oil wells burned in the distance. The adrenaline and fear started to well up inside her. It was 3 a.m. Courtney had her night goggles on so everything looked large and scary. "I saw movement by the fire. My Sergeant told me to slow down. I didn't know what to do." Then she just stopped as they reached some Marines by the road.

Her captain had indeed led them in the wrong direction, into a Marine/ Iraqi combat zone near Basra. Also in that area were British coalition troops. "The Marines told us that we should not be riding out in this area with our high beams on. They could have lit us up [shot us]. We could have been a threat to them." The Marines gave the convoy members gas for their vehicles because the vehicles left in the convoy were running nearly on empty.

Once the convey started driving again, no one trusted the captain's directions, least of all the warrant officer who verbally chastised the captain for getting them lost and nearly killed. Now, following the directions of the warrant officer, they caught up with their main rear advance unit and made their way to Bagdad. Their ordeal had been a twenty-three-hour nerve-racking trip. It was a situation eerily similar to that of the convoy attacked in March 2003, when Shoshanna Johnson and members of her unit were captured.

DUTY, DEDICATION, DEATH: AFRICAN AMERICAN SERVICEWOMEN'S ULTIMATE SACRIFICE

Since they did have an integral role in serving with military forces during the twentieth and twenty-first centuries, African American servicewomen have frequently given their lives in the line of duty. Three African American women were killed during Operation Desert Storm, while twenty died during the Iraqi conflict. The death count will no doubt rise as women serve in Afghanistan. At this writing, that conflict is scheduled to end for American forces in 2014. That certainly will not be the end of the danger for African American women in military conflicts. Military specialists and leaders believe that in the near future the ban on women serving in infantry, armor and special forces units should eventually be lifted even if done so in increments.

In early 2012, military advisors recommended to Congress that women be formally assigned directly to a battalion, a unit of from three hundred to fifteen hundred personnel. They could serve in intelligence and communications. They could be military police and medics. Formally, women could not be assigned to these types of jobs in the Army and the Marines, but they could do the same work in a support capacity. Women served well during Operation Desert Storm and the Iraqi conflict—so well, in fact, that government review of their collective service opened doors for them to further integrate into combat roles.

These rule changes opened 14,000 jobs to women. For example, in May, 2012, the Army allowed women to take combat support military roles. They could be artillery mechanics, M1 Abrams tank systems maintainers, field artillery fire finder radar operators, multiple launch rocket system crew members, and multiple launch rocket system operations fire detection specialists. In July 2012, the Army signed up its first female recruit to train for work as a Bradley fighting vehicle systems maintainer.

The Marines plan to allow forty-five female officers and noncommissioned officers to join artillery tank and combat engineer battalions. The goal is for these women to fit seamlessly into an evolving command climate that will no longer follow antiquated, gender limiting philosophies and practices. As part of a Marine study to determine the feasibility of women becoming ground combat leaders, two female officers volunteered to undergo training in the Marines' rigorous thirteen-week infantry course, considered by some to be one of the toughest courses in the Corps. Both dropped out of the course, along with twenty-eight men. The course typically has a 20 percent to 25 percent attrition rate.

These new steps to allow women to serve in these positions are still not enough for some. Right now, women are still barred from serving in some crucial combat units, and that ban excludes women from leading certain combat units. Two women in the Army Reserves, Command Sergeant Major

Jane P. Baldwin from Florida and Colonel Ellen L. Haring of Bristow, Virginia, took exception to the government's refusal to remove the ban on women serving in combat. They filed a lawsuit in Federal District Court in Washington, D.C., against the Army and the Department of Defense, the first such lawsuit to address this issue. Their lawsuit contended that they were being discriminated against because of their gender. This discrimination was preventing them from attaining leadership in combat units, thus denying them the chance for promotion to senior officer and enlisted ranks positions. Both women felt that their current positions were limited to support jobs, despite the fact that Baldwin had served twenty years and Haring twenty-eight. They argued that attaching women to combat units was not enough if women were not going to get full credit and benefits for actual service. Their suit claimed that this ban on women in combat is unconstitutional in that it prohibits women from earning equal pay, comparative retirement benefits, and future advancements. The suit also stated that the ban causes Haring, Baldwin, and other servicewomen to suffer invidious discriminatory treatment in a work environment that institutionalizes the unequal treatment of women solely because of their sex.

In November 2012, the American Civil Liberties Union, along with four servicewomen, filed another lawsuit against the Defense Department. Hegar vs. Panetta, was filed in U.S. District Court in the Northern District of California. Echoing the challenges of the other suit, the ACLU claimed that combat restrictions forged against women solely because of their sex were unconstitutional. The ACLU claims that "nearly a century after women first earned the right of suffrage, the combat exclusion policy still denies women a core component of full citizenship—serving on equal footing in the military defense of our nation."

Action taken by Secretary of Defense Leon Panetta may make these lawsuits moot. In January 2013, Secretary Panetta removed the military's ban on women serving in combat. This opening will allow to women serve in hundreds of thousands of front line positions as early as the end of 2013. Eventually the repeal of the 1994 law that stopped women from serving in small combat units may let women serve in the Navy Seals and Delta forces, but not right away.

There is no prediction regarding the success of these lawsuits. If they are ultimately successful, the impact on African American women who serve in the military would be considerable. This dramatic action might open up 230,000 jobs to women who serve in the Army and the Marines. African American women are currently operating in combat/support roles in the Afghanistan War. Black servicewomen will continue their stalwart Sistahs of Defense role in the protection of the nation's interests and worldwide mission against terrorism and the insurgents who advance it.

NOTES

1. There was a close connection between the base and nearby town, which would be saddened the following year when the base closed. The last plane took off from the runway March 6, 1992. The plane was christened The City of Blytheville in honor of the community. See a synopsis base history at www.mcagov.com/history/eaker-air-force-base.

2. Lieutenant General Santarelli during this time was commander of the U.S. Central Command Air Forces (Forward) and of the 4404t h Composite Wing (Provisional), Saudi Arabia. Information on the general and his career can be found at www.af.mil/information/bios/ bio_print.asp?bioID=7033.

3. See the Central Command Web site at www.centcom.mil.

Chapter Four

My Child Left Behind

*The Family and Child Care Challenges Faced
by African American Gulf War Servicewomen*

I did not want to go, but I did. If I remember correctly, none of the African American women in my unit took hardships [dependency or hardship discharge]. We all deployed.
—Kim Hatcher, Army E-4, Operation Desert Storm

The menu for our Mother's Day dinner was corn dogs and French fries. I stayed in my cot, cried, and went to sleep. On Father's Day, they served steak and lobster. I felt so unappreciated as a woman and a mother. I am still angry about that.
—Maria Quillan, Navy E-5, Operation Iraqi Freedom

Our nation owes a greater deal to what I call the "power behind the power," the families of all those who are serving. While our men and women in uniform may be called to pay the highest price, their families, and particularly their spouses make a considerable sacrifice as well.
—United States Secretary of Defense Robert M. Gates, 2008

I do not know how long he had been quietly standing in the dark shadows of my small bedroom, watching me sleep. At some point, I must have heard him move, because I stirred out of my slumber and partially opened my eyes. I was not afraid. Somehow, I must have known he was not one of those ghoulish nightmare characters that had frequently haunted my dreams for the past few months. Rubbing the sleep from my eyes, I sat up and peered intently into the face of the dark-skinned mustached man who now stood in front of my bed. He looked worried when he finally spoke and anxiously asked me, "Do you know who I am?"

When I jumped into his outstretched arms and yelled, "Daddy," that anxious look was quickly replaced with a broad grin and a crushing bear hug. That night after being gone for a year, my Army father had returned to our Seattle home from the first of several deployments and temporary assignments. It was 1960, and I was three years old. That is my first and most endearing memory of military family life as an enlisted soldier's child, growing up in the 1960s and 1970s.

As I grew older, my memories ceased being idyllic and became increasingly bittersweet. In my young mind, the Army became an omnipresent, overbearing green ogre that controlled every facet of our family's existence, twenty-four hours a day, seven days a week.

In 1956, when my dad was a young bachelor from Hogansville, Georgia, he raised his right hand and joined the Army. His level of commitment to his oath did not lessen when he married and took on family responsibilities the following year. In those days, the running joke was that, if the Army had wanted a young soldier to have a family, it would have issued him one. Some wondered if this statement was even a joke. He had to be able to pack his duffle bag, shoulder his rifle, and leave his family at a moment's notice. Sometimes, that meant leaving for places unknown for an indeterminate amount of time.

Without exception, the Army came first in our lives, which often meant less "Daddy time" for me and my two siblings. Of the three children, I took this perceived military intrusion in our family's life especially hard. By the time I was ten, after experiencing some of these military-induced family separations, it grew harder for me to fully enjoy his homecoming from yet another deployment, because I knew he would have to leave us again. To quell my fears about his leaving, I began compulsively looking for any advance sign or clue about an impending departure. I even eavesdropped on my parents' private conversations. Sometimes, my snooping paid off, leaving me with mixed emotions. My anxiety only intensified whenever I managed to find out he was leaving before I was supposed to "officially" know.

Predeployment time was stressful for all of us. In the early part of my dad's military career, we did not live on the Army post he was usually assigned to (Fort Lawton, Seattle, Washington), so we did not get to undergo the collective unit pre-deployment rituals most military families of that era experienced. My parents tried their best to prepare us, however. To best plan their strategy for how and what to tell the kids, they went behind closed doors, sometimes for hours to discuss "Daddy's upcoming Army trip." When my dad and mom emerged, each child was told what he or she could understand, handle, and needed to know about the trip.

I had to endure sitting through my dad telling me, "You are the oldest. I expect you to be good and help your mom while I am gone." He always had to add the "be good" part, because he knew that as soon as he left, I would most likely be anything but that. He knew that I usually took his leaving especially hard, but he did not know that I deeply feared for his life and safety. He did not know about the constant nightmares I had about not having a daddy at home to protect us and about the stomachaches I suffered imagining him suffering a horrible fate from some imagined enemy. He *did* know that, when he was gone, I underwent repeated child psychiatric consultations and evaluations. Mom received concerned phone calls and home visits from teachers, elementary school counselors, and social workers regarding my "aberrant, aggressive behavior and perpetual acting out" in my elementary school classrooms. However, he was just as perplexed about the root cause of my behavior as those mental health and educational experts who endeavored to treat me. In the 1960s, empirical studies on the effect of military deployments on children were not yet a priority in scholarship. Those types of studies would only begin to emerge with more frequency after Desert Storm.

Despite my obvious separation anxiety issues, dad still expected me to "salute smartly and be a good soldier's daughter." Unfortunately, those dreaded "Daddy's got to leave" talks never got any easier for either of us. Truthfully, I never wanted them to get any easier for him because I did not want to make his leaving us stress-free. Doing my youthful best to complicate the departure process, I always asked him where he was going, why he had to go, and when he would return. Sometimes, my questions got even more pointed and in retrospect, for him, more agonizing. Will you be here for my birthday? Will you be here for Christmas? I knew he did not have the answers I really wanted to hear, but I kept asking the questions anyway, vainly hoping that maybe someday he would.

Sometimes my dad would be gone for a month, three months, six months, or even a year. Whenever he was gone, time stood unbearably still for me. As I grew older, I saw the toll the separations took on my mom, but to her credit as a good soldier's wife, she tried to remain positive for the sake of the children. Only in my adult years, and with incessant prodding from me, did she even grudgingly confess the true difficulty of the herculean task of being mother *and* father. We still laugh about the time when we were ten, eight, and six, that we all caught the flu at the same time. Mom had to run back and forth administrating healing aid and comfort. Once she devised a clever cuisine scheme, baking four Cornish game hens and telling us with a straight face that they were our own baby turkeys. She wanted to avoid cooking the traditional big meal my dad usually made for our Thanksgivings.

She took a variety of jobs in order to supplement the meager enlisted pay my dad received. Before organized day care became an affordable option, she had to rely on a bevy of babysitters, some with greater child nurturing skills than others. Fortunately, my mom's family provided a support system nucleus. My godfather, who was a church pastor and a teenaged uncle served as dedicated surrogate male role models, but I still missed my dad.

One thing was certain: He too despised the forced separations and the immense pain they caused his wife and children. So, like the silent shadow that had crept into his three-year-old daughter's bedroom that night, sometimes he would just as quietly slip away to the new temporary military assignment while we slept or were at school. This stealthy departure technique ultimately proved to be the least painful way for him to leave and avoid saying "goodbyes" to the two young daughters and son. After my father became a mid-level noncommissioned officer (Staff Sergeant, E6). His military forays away from us became less frequent, and by the time I reached my early adolescence, they had ceased. The shadow had returned home to us, this time to stay. Actually, my family was fortunate. My dad was not re-assigned or deployed nearly as often as were many other Army fathers who served during the Vietnam War era.

Today, the separation issues and other challenges military service members and their families face have become more complex. Men are not the only ones deploying; increasing numbers of servicewomen are also deploying, leaving their spouses and children behind. A review of Department of Defense demographic statistics indicates a completely new pattern. In 1990, 40,000 U.S. servicewomen deployed in support of Desert Shield/Desert Storm. A decade later, more than 170,000 women had deployed to Iraq or Afghanistan. Rising deployment numbers for both sexes have also greatly affected other family members. As of June 2008, there were 1.8 million deployments. Since September 2001, 900,000 service members with children have deployed and currently 234,000 children have at least one parent deployed overseas. Current Department of Defense statistics state that almost 40 percent of military servicewomen are parents, compared to 44 percent of military men.[1] Other statistics gleaned from the *Department of Defense 2011 Demographics Report* of *Military Families* indicate even more children of all ages could be affected by this new deployment pattern. Over 1 million (1.7) military children of active duty parents are between the ages of birth and twenty-three years. The largest group of children is between birth and five years old (481,103), followed by the six to eleven (368,850) and twelve to eighteen (279,319) age groups. For the select reserves, six to fourteen years of age is the largest children's group (327,342), followed by birth to five years (175,401) and fifteen to eighteen years (125,284).[2] In the twenty-first century, the growing number of deploying servicewomen has forced Americans to re-evaluate the existing ban on women serving in combat zones.

In the past four years, Gallup, *USA Today*, CNN, and Roper opinion polls have consistently showed a slight majority of Americans supporting lifting the ban. Americans, however, still have balked at having servicewomen who are mothers deploy and fight in actual combat zones. Both of these views are consistent with those found in a 1991 Associated Press poll. In it, 64 percent of those surveyed said they thought it was "unacceptable for the United States to send women with young children to the war zone."

Despite this national reluctance to send mothers into combat, many African American mothers with young children served in Desert Storm. U.S. Air Force Staff Sergeant Hearther Overstreet, now retired, was one of those women. Before the war, she was assigned to Tinker Air Force Base in Oklahoma. She served as an aircraft fuel systems technician for the Air Force's Airborne Warning and Control System E3 Sentry (better known as the AWACS), a military plane that, from the air, provides commanders with all-weather surveillance and command, control, and communications needed to plan battle campaigns.

Hearther routinely deployed with her AWACS unit several times a year for thirty to forty-five days each to support U.S. and NATO military exercises and training activities. In 1990, one of those temporary duty assignments (TDYs) took her to Riyadh, Saudi Arabia, at the onset of Desert Shield. Her usual thirty-to-forty-five-day stint passed with no word on returning, but she hardly noticed. Long TDYs (temporary duties) to the Middle East were nothing new.

When she found out that this particular trip to Riyadh was actually her unit's foray into Operation Desert Shield, she settled into her temporary quarters at Escon Village with other women from her unit. Escon Village was made up of housing units that the Saudis had built for the nomadic Bedouins. She jumped quickly into battle preparation work. When she was not on the flight line or in an aircraft maintenance hangar, she took her place among throngs of U.S. and coalition forces personnel who were filling sandbags and making bunkers for the impending war. Sometimes the realization that she was in a war zone was so overwhelming, she hardly could believe that she was supposed to be there. But there she was, right in the thick of it.

On January 17, 1991, the day Operation Desert Storm started, she helped launch the first E3A into the fray. "My spouse was on that flight, but I did not know for the first three days."

Her daily regimen was briefly interrupted on the night before the war began as the Deputy Commander of Maintenance (DCM) called all of the 100 unit members together. She would not forget his words: If they repeated anything he told them, they would have to be killed. Since the DCM had a 9mm pistol holstered menacingly on his hip at the time, she did not doubt the implied seriousness of his threat.

After pausing to let that statement sink in, he quickly launched into a rousing wartime pep talk. "The war is about to start, so we could be here for the duration. It could be six months to a year. We're gonna have to do our best, and we're gonna win," he exhorted. As he continued rallying his troops to "victory," Hearther remembered, his voice became white noise and quickly faded into the background. From the moment he had dropped that verbal bombshell about killing them, few bothered listening to the rest. Many of them were in a state of shock. "We just stood and looked at each other," Hearther recalled. When the DCM finally walked away, pandemonium erupted. "Some of the guys were yelling, screaming; there were tears. But the six of us girls [the only women assigned to this unit] did fine. We did not cry or say a word."

When Operation Desert Storm rolled in pre-dawn January 17, 1991, she helped launch the first E3A into the fray. "My spouse was on that flight, but I did not know for the first three days," Hearther stated incredulously. Hearther was determined to remain focused on her job. Failure was not an option. As the first woman *and* the first woman of color in her Air Force career field, Hearther could not afford to rest easy on her hard-earned laurels. From the onset of her career, she constantly had to prove to her resentful subordinates and colleagues that she could turn a wrench and "fix a broken bird" with the best of them. Proving she could supervise and confidently call aircraft maintenance shots in the throes of Desert Storm became her ultimate test. "I had to show I could do the job, or not do it. I could not fudge or fake it," she recalled. Despites the dangers, she knew she had to focus on continuing to prove her worth as an aircraft maintenance technician and survive whatever came her way.

All around her, Patriot missiles were positioned in launch mode. She breathed in the heavy acrid smoke from the 600 burning oilfields in Kuwait and wondered about her health. She cringed every time the warning alarms went off, and she had to don her mask and chemical gear. All types of coalition aircraft launched and took off, nonstop. "I felt the ground shaking under my feet when the airplanes took off," she said. Hearther also had to live with the daily threat of launching AWACS aircraft and not knowing if her crewmember husband was aboard or, if he was, whether he would he come back. In the midst of all of that tension, she found one unusual way of relieving the unrelenting daily pressure: She became her own combat manicurist. "I wore a lot of nail polish to keep my nerves steady." Hearther adapted a coolly philosophical survivalist mindset about the whole ordeal. "Either you could do the job or you couldn't," she decided. Until her unit left for Oklahoma in March 1991, she was integral in making sure that 845 AWACS sorties were flown without a maintenance hitch.

One event almost threatened to derail her focus—a sick four-year-old son back home. Hearther's husband was the primary family childcare back up when she went TDY. Although they were in the same flying unit, he was initially home when she first left for Saudi Arabia. However, since her husband was still an aircrew member on flying status, he could be deployed at any time, and this time he was. She had not been gone long when he got his call to deploy. A serious child care crisis had been averted when a unit co-worker stepped in.

That worked until the Overstreets' son became mysteriously ill. Panic ensued. "My co-worker's wife happened to be pregnant. My son got sick. They did not know what the cause was," Hearther explained. The co-worker, afraid that the Overstreets' son's undiagnosed illness might somehow endanger his wife's pregnancy, called Hearther's husband and told him to come and get their son.

It was fortunate that her husband could quickly get emergency leave back to the states. "My son was misdiagnosed and was on his death bed. He almost died from an untreated ear infection," she said. Even though their son was gravely ill, her husband was not allowed to remain home with him. With a war on, he had to come back on flying status as quickly as possible. His mother quickly stepped in and became her grandson's caretaker until Hearther and her husband returned from Desert Storm.

Somberly looking back on her son's near-death experience, Hearther said she understood why her husband deliberately kept her in the dark about her son's condition—there was nothing she could have done in Saudi Arabia but worry. "When I found out about it, I developed tunnel vision and remained totally focused on my job. I did not talk to my son until I was in Germany on my way home from the war." Only after she arrived home months later and was reunited with her son, did she really allow herself to think about what she would have done had he died. She said she still thinks about it.

Kim Hatcher, a junior noncommissioned officer (E-4), was one of the 48 percent of African American Army servicewomen who deployed during Desert Storm. The military personnel specialist was shocked to learn shortly before the Thanksgiving-Christmas holiday season that her personnel and casualty reports unit would shortly deploy from Bamberg, Germany, to Saudi Arabia in support of Desert Shield. The shock was compounded when her unit's first sergeant gave the parents three days to take their children stateside to relatives or responsible guardians and return for the deployment. Kim's husband, also at Bamberg, was in another soon-to-deploy Army unit, so the quick trip responsibility fell on her.

Before she left Germany, Kim and the other military parents in the unit were told that those who could not make adequate childcare arrangements would be allowed to apply for an Army hardship discharge. Many quickly jumped at the opportunity, but Kim hesitated. In 1992, the Department of Defense rescinded this hardship discharge policy for all of the services. All single military service members and those married to other service members had to have a workable childcare plan in place that would allow them to deploy or be re-assigned worldwide.

"I was surprised at the people who actually decided to get out of the Army. Most of them were folks I thought were lifers, true Army types," she said. As she mulled the options, one African American male sergeant sneeringly said to her, "I suppose you are going to bail out too?" For Kim, the decision to deploy or get the discharge was tough. However, she was no quitter. A self-described strong black woman, she had come this far in her career and decided she would go this one last step. She would deploy, even it meant leaving her children behind. "I did not want to go, but I did. If I remember correctly, none of the African American women in my unit took hardships. We all deployed," she said proudly. Reluctant to part with them, she kept the boys with her in Germany as long as she could. The day after Thanksgiving, she took her four-year-old and eighteen-month-old sons to Maryland and left them with her mother and extended family. Blissfully unaware of the trip's true purpose, the boys were very excited, she said. She, however, was devastated. She wondered if she had made the right decision. She said her quick goodbyes to her sons and other family members and went back in Germany, ready to deploy. Her unit left shortly before Christmas.

Kim knew her children would be safe and well taken care of in her mom's good hands. On the surface, that realization helped make her decision easier. After all, her mother had single-handedly raised a close-knit family of seven children. As expected, while Kim and her husband were deployed, her mother provided similar care for her grandsons, this time with extended family assistance. When her mother worked during the day, a family friend babysat. Kim's other sisters and brothers and their families provided care. Her husband's family frequently called to check on the boys, always offering to lend their support. Still, even with all of this tender loving care given freely by her relatives, Kim said she felt horrible being away from her children. To ease that pain, she called and talked to her sons whenever possible, but even those brief contacts did not soothe her anguish. The time zone difference made it even harder for her to talk to them when they were awake. However, each time she called, her mother would wake them up to talk to her because, her mother maintained, "They need to hear your voice." Although Kim felt great talking to them, she also felt guilty because her youngest son would not go back to sleep. It was even harder for Kim's husband to call and talk to the boys. He could only do it a few times because it really tore him up inside, especially when the oldest one would always ask him "When are you coming back?" Kim said. The overwhelming guilt Kim experienced as a mother separated from her children was, as, one study of military parents found, more complicated because "women have traditionally borne the responsibility for child care and have a strong commitment to their maternal roles."[3]

Kim was not the only mother in her new Desert Storm unit. The unit consisted mostly of African American and Hispanic Army servicewomen from Kim's home unit and active duty troops from Fort Riley, Kansas.

Throughout the war, their tears flowed freely about anything and everything, especially when it came to missing their children, she said. "We cried if you got a letter that had a picture of your baby in it, and it looked like your baby had grown ten times bigger since the last picture you got." The collective sadness these women shared about leaving their children behind also helped them bond and forget the harshness of the war, she said. The stronger ones helped the weaker get through. "We understood what the others were going through, and we were there for each other," she said.

The dangers of war quickly hit close to home for Kim. One night while she was on shift, her sergeant major came in with the news that the 82nd Engineering, her husband's unit, had suffered some causalities and fatalities. She said she immediately became a "basket case" because there was no word on who had been injured or who had died. It was a long nerve wracking night for her because official word did not come in that her husband was not injured until later on that morning. Even though she was relieved that her husband was safe, she was still sad because she knew those people in his unit who had become casualties.

She found herself in personal dangerous situations several times during the war. While on guard duty, she had to wear full armor gear. Explosives often fell around her. That danger gave her the stark realization that "We really are at war." She had been a tough person, but she freely admits to crying a lot. Hatcher was sent to a variety of places in the combat theater during her deployment. While in Riyadh for the last two weeks of her deployment, a severe sand storm collapsed the tent she was living in. She was almost buried in sand. She was dragged out of the tent and taken to a military hospital unit. She awoke to a new sense horror when she realized she was in a hospital cot next to dead soldiers.

When Kim returned to the United States, she was met at the airport by a throng of screaming, sign-waving, balloon-carrying family members and friends. Kim, however, wanted only to see her sons. Scanning the large cheering crowd, she spotted them and ran to claim them. But the long-anticipated joyful reunion did not materialize as she had dreamed. While it did not take very long for her four-year-old to recognize and go to her, the youngest one was frightened and confused. "He had a hard time," she sadly explained. After a few anxious days of wondering if he would ever remember her, he finally warmed up. "It was like he said, 'Oh, I know who you are now,'" she said, the relief still evident in her voice. The bittersweet homecoming and her youngest son's fearful reaction left an indelible impression on her. His brief rejection of her deeply reinforced the guilt she felt for leaving her children behind in the first place. Added to that guilt, a couple of questions nagged at her conscience: What would happen if the Army forced her and her husband to deploy at the same time and leave their children again? All during the war, Kim admitted, she wondered what would happen to her sons if she and/or her husband were killed. She knew both families would have stepped up to take care of them as they had during Desert Storm. No doubt, her mother would have volunteered to raise them herself. Kim did not wanted her mother to face the necessity of raising orphaned grandsons, even if she was willing. It did not take her long to make the obvious choice of leaving the Army. Kim said she does not regret making that decision. Her time in the Army and during Desert Storm was "precious," she said. It ultimately taught her how to appreciate things that people routinely take for granted, like the love and support of your family and the love of your children. Kim walked away from a promising Army career and has never looked back because of her love for her sons and the unconditional love she received from them.

As told in chapter 3, Specialist Four Patricia Johnson served with the military police in Panama during the Just Cause conflict. Later she became a military postal clerk specialist.

Patricia was a single parent whose first son was in kindergarten when she got the call to deploy to Saudi Arabia for Desert Shield/Desert Storm. Since his birth, she had always turned to her parents for long-term childcare support when she had to leave him because of her military obligations. However, leaving her son with them this time was far more devastating. "It was awful. I cried every day because of the fact of having to leave on Christmas Eve 1990. It [deploying] was heart-wrecking," she said. Once she arrived in Saudi Arabia in early January 1991, she worked hard to keep in touch with him, in order to ease the pain and guilt. She called home almost every day. "Every chance I got, I called my family. I wrote letters, and, oh man, I ran my daddy's phone bill up so high while I was there, I had to make him out an allotment," she said, lightly laughing at the memory.

A September 2005 report from the National Military Family Association, based on a survey regarding family dynamics during deployment found that maintaining consistent communication with family (e.g., through e-mail, phone calls, regular mail, and packages) is paramount to preserving military family unity and keeping up troop morale.[4] However, using calling cards (expensive but vital) and getting the intermittent fifteen-minute-a-week morale call was not always enough for Patricia. Even with her fervent attempts to keep in contact with her son, the separation was unbearable. After being deployed for seven months, Patricia came home one month earlier than the rest of her unit when she discovered that she was four months pregnant. His second child's father was a close friend she had met at Fort Leonard, Maryland, while they were both going through the Army's military police training schools. They reunited during the war.

Like the others with young children, she had a long and bumpy adjustment period with her son when she came home. When she first saw him, he was confused and did not recognize her. Patricia, however, immediately understood why. "He was a little distant, and he had to get used to me. He did not understand what was going on. I had been gone for seven months to Desert Storm and for most of the other four of the five years of his young life," she explained. He had become used to her not being home. She worked hard to change that. Over the years, her efforts to erase the pain of separation appear to have paid off. She said she is now very close to both of her sons.

A Desert Storm deployment actually proved to be a godsend for Senior Airman Carolyn Morgan. In the early stages of her military career, she joined the Air National Guard in Wisconsin and played in a military band until she injured her fingers. After the injury, she held a variety of military jobs. She was one of the first women in her Guard unit to drive military vehicles for its transportation squadron. Finally she settled into being a cook. In 1985, she joined the active duty Air Force to get more discipline in her life. Five years later, she was a junior NCO (an E-4). She faced conflict in her marriage and decided to volunteer to serve in Desert Storm, even though it meant leaving her eighteen-month-old daughter and six-month-old son behind. As painful as the decision was for her, she said, it ultimately saved her life.

In 1990, Carolyn moved with her civilian husband and two young children from Wisconsin to Shaw Air Force Base, South Carolina, to get a new start for their lives. Carolyn admitted that she went into the move knowing it would be a calculated risk. At that time, military interracial couples like Carolyn and her white husband had the option of passing up assignments to Southern states known for racial intolerance. Despite her fears about encountering even more racial prejudice than she had before, she remained hopeful. The prospect of having a fresh beginning with her husband and children eventually won out over those fears.

Unfortunately, the move did not bring about the change she had envisioned for her family. Her husband became an absentee alcoholic spouse and father who adamantly refused to care and provide for her and their children. "My marriage wasn't good. I loved my children, and I was a single mom anyway. . . . He wasn't there. It was tough." In frequent fits of vengeance and anger, her husband attempted to destroy her career, she said. To preserve her sanity, her career, and her life, she decided that she had to leave him and quickly, even if meant sacrificing her time with her children. Carolyn devised an escape plan.

She knew she would not be able to depend upon her husband to care for the children, and her family was far away. However, Carolyn already had someone who was providing good childcare for her children. "We had a babysitter who was really wonderful, and she really took care of the kids. She started babysitting before I left." Carolyn's escape plan was expensive. "I paid her a lot of money to babysit my children. She ended up buying a new truck and new furniture for the sitter's home. That's how much I paid out in babysitting fees." Entrusting her children to the babysitter, Carolyn said goodbye and deployed. Upon arrival in the war zone on August 10, 1990, she was assigned to Abu Dubai, a large U.S. rest and recreation station where she served primarily as a night shift headquarters message courier.

She desperately missed her children. Like the other military mothers around her, she attempted to keep in touch with them by sending photos, packages, and letters, and calling when she could. She even sent them a videotape. However, eight months later, when she returned to South Carolina, she had to re-introduce herself as "Mommy." Initially, it was not easy, she noted. "My son [who was fourteen months old] did not know who I was. He had no idea who I was." Her initial reunion with her daughter was a little better but somewhat humorous. "My daughter announced to me that she was 'a big girl' and that she wanted to go to school. She had grown up and was quite mature. She was definitely ready to go to pre-school." Carolyn's minor shock over the change in her children's independence is common. Family systems tend to change when military members are deployed. Upon return, returning parents must acknowledge and accept this change.

Her marital situation did not change, however. Carolyn's ex-husband was still largely absent and not supportive. He had formally moved out while she was gone. He lived nearby but provided no support to her and the children. His move gave Carolyn the much-needed impetus to make additional escape plans from this painful marital morass. Immediately, she threw herself into cutting off all remaining ties with him and re-acquainting herself with her children. Looking for another fresh geographical start, she applied for a recruiter's position and ended up in Rhode Island. Once in her new location, she worked tirelessly to become re-acquainted with her children. "I totally absorbed myself into my kids. If I was not at work, I would be with my kids doing everything together," she said.

Inexplicably, she admitted, while in Rhode Island she and her estranged husband attempted a brief but unsuccessful marital reunion. In the end, Carolyn, now formally a single parent, moved on, her children and career her new main priorities. Looking back on that turbulent time, Carolyn said she never regretted "running away" to any dangers Desert Storm posed from the real danger in her volatile marital relationship. "It was hard for me, but I needed to go." For her, that act of desperation was the right thing to do to ensure that she would ultimately be with her children.

Twenty-year-old Army Specialist Courtney Salter left her toddler son for almost a year when her battalion deployed to Kuwait and Bagdad during Operation Iraqi Freedom in 2003. Barely out of basic and advanced individual training (AIT), supply specialist Salter underwent grueling twelve to fifteen hours a day pre-deployment training for four months. This became a problem when it came to getting quality childcare and spending time with her son. A single parent, her childcare support system plan was not ideal. She had a rocky relationship with her son's father, who showed little or no interest in the toddler. The only time he nominally got involved was at his parents' insistence. She was not willing to turn her son over to the biological father nor his family, yet she had no other long-term options. Courtney's fiancé could not take her son because he had an upcoming assignment to South Korea. Neither her mother nor her two sisters could afford to take care of her son. "My son was two and one-half when I deployed. He had to go to his grandparents for about three or four months prior to my actual deployment because of the training exercises and long work hours. It was hard being away from him, but I felt it was a little easier to deal with because he was so young and he probably wouldn't remember our separation later," she said.

Her time spent away from her son was miserable. She was homesick and consumed with guilt for leaving her son. She constantly wondered how long her deployment would last. Would she be home to celebrate his third birthday?

Ramon Hinjosa, Sberna Hinojosa, and Robin Hognas contend that military members forced to rely on communicating with family members through security censored long distance telephone calls and equally expurgated letters can suffer because of the restricted communication flow.[5] While deployed, Courtney Salter frequently sent home pictures and letters so he would not forget her, but even this attempt at having "open and free flowing communication" with her young son proved daunting. Whenever she could, she would call his paternal grandparents and talk to him, a task that proved to be frustrating for her. "I contacted him as much as I could, but he did not like talking on the phone," she noted. Her siblings served as her liaison, checking up on her son for her when they could. True to form, her son's biological father did very little to make her feel that her son was thriving and happy living with his parents. He briefly contacted her only once to let her know about her son's well-being. "He sent me a two-line letter," she said bitterly.

As it got closer to her son's birthday, Salter began to ask her commander when her battalion was returning stateside. Unlike the Air Force, which had a set 120-day deployment rotation schedule for its troops, the army leaned toward a changeover when the mission was "complete" at the beginning of Operation Iraqi Freedom. "I said to my commander, "my baby's birthday is on such and such a day in June. Will we be home by then? Obviously, he felt sorry for me so he told me we would be home by June 19. That day came and went and we were still there," Courtney noted.

Her battalion returned to Georgia in July 2003. She arrived excited, ready to see her baby, yet nervously wondering if he would remember her. "When I got back, I saw my mother and my sister, and then I saw my baby. He talked to me from the very moment he saw me. He knew who I was. He was a pretty hip little baby." Courtney immediately sped away with her son and spent a bit of uninterrupted quality time. She admits to spoiling him while they bonded and he adjusted to being back with her. "I let him get away with just about everything for a while," she confessed.

Two years later, Sergeant Salter's unit was ready to deploy to Iraq again. She was now married, and her husband was serving in the same unit. Since both of them would deploy, Courtney once again faced tough long-term childcare decisions. Her husband knew he would deploy since he was a career soldier. He decided this decision had to be one she made on her own.

Fortunately, the Salters had more time to weigh the pros and cons of Courtney staying in the military and the implications of long-term childcare, but that did not make the decision any easier. "Should I deploy with my husband and be his companion through the hard times, or should I stay with my son, who would be entering kindergarten? I had missed his first words, first steps, first day of day care and his first and third birthdays—all because of my Army obligation. Torn between the two, I felt I would lose no matter what I chose. After months of consideration, I decided that, while my husband needed me, my son needed me more."

Her husband fully supported her decision. "He later admitted that I made the right choice because twelve months was too long for someone else to have my son." Courtney got out of the Army's Family Care Plan and never looked back on her decision. "After my son started kindergarten and began reading, my husband told me that he was glad that at least one of us was there to be a part of that achievement."

Mothers with small children were not the only ones who felt the impact of leaving loved ones behind. Even in all of her busyness while in Bagdad, Gwendolyn found herself missing her college-age brother. She had raised him as her own son since her mother died in 1993. Because of illness, her father was not able to care for him when her mother died, so Gwendolyn took on the parenting responsibility. Her brother played football for North Dakota State University and was in his last year of playing eligibility when she deployed. Knowing how special football was to him, Gwendolyn said she was proud that, prior to her deployment, she had been able to attend almost all of his home and away games. "I only missed about six of his games. It was not an easy task to attend them because I was always traveling with my civilian job."

When she was home, she called him at least five times a week, but in Bagdad she had to improvise. "Each week we were given two fifteen-minute morale calls. I would call him before his games and after his games." Her brother's games were also broadcast on the Internet. With time zone differences, his games would start at 5 a.m. Baghdad time. Even at that pre-dawn hour, Gwendolyn would get up and try to listen to as many games as she could. "After the games, they would interview him, and he would give a shout out to me and my troops. We always got a big kick out of that." Making that early morning radio listening time sacrifice turned out to be critical to keeping up with her brother's football games, because she saw only the final game of his senior year after she returned home from Iraq in November 2003.

Navy E-5 Maria Quillan was a longtime member of a large cargo-handling unit when she deployed from January to June in 2003. A special education teacher in civilian life, she had served in the active duty Army for three years and had sixteen years as a reservist assigned to Little Creek Amphibious Base in Virginia Beach, Virginia. Maria said she could drive any type of truck or vehicle the Navy had in its transportation pool. She knew cargo handling and loading, but she had used this skill only in peacetime.

That was about to change. In 2003, a call to an active duty deployment shocked the fifty-five-year-old grandmother, who was in the twilight of her military career. She was one year from military retirement.

When she first heard that her unit was deploying to Kuwait, she was not overly concerned. She was confident that she was not going to deploy because of her documented health issues. So it was much to her surprise when she did deploy to Kuwait in support of Operation Iraqi Freedom. "I had swollen joints, arthritis, and was menopausal, and they still cleared me to deploy," she said.

Not only was the deployment physically painful, but for the next six months, Marie had to endure separation from her three grandchildren. The hardest separation she endured, however, was not being able to see her son, who was in a deployed unit in Iraq. Mother's Day 2003 was especially hard for her. "I was feeling bad because my son Douglas could not visit me on his twenty-seventh birthday, which was May 6, or on Mother's Day, May 10. To make matters worse, the menu for our Mother's Day dinner was corn dogs and French fries. I stayed in my cot, cried, and went to sleep. On Father's Day, they served steak and lobster. I felt so unappreciated as a woman and a mother. I am still angry about that," she declared.

Determined to keep her connections to her family ever present in her mind, Marie visited a Kuwaiti elementary school. "I saw children playing and heard them singing and laughing. This was a memorable moment for me because I hadn't seen or heard this innocent joy for five months."

Even if she could not see her son, Marie could help others at Camp Patriot connect with their families. Marie set up and operated the camp's Internet café, which quickly became a very popular gathering spot. While operating the café, she also took time to provide wise counsel, solace, and comfort to scared young troops, many of them mothers away from their young children for the first time. In no time, the grandmother became the camp's designated "mother figure." Her mothering role helped pass the time and paid off when she finally was able to see her son. "An African American Army first sergeant pulled some strings and allowed my son to come and visit me. It was the best thing that happened to me the whole time I was there."

Separation from children, wondering if they would ever see them again, was unanimously remembered by African American women interviewed as the most stressful, painful aspect of deployment to Desert Storm in 1991. SCUD missile attacks, donning cumbersome chemical warfare gear in blazing heat, and fighting losing battles against biting, blowing sand paled in comparison to the fear of being rebuffed upon the return home by children who did not remember their mother or were angry that she had left them. Mothers had anxious thoughts about their children becoming war orphans. However, all of the women knew that if they could just get home from the war and see their children, everything would work out. Their families, no matter how long it took, would heal and remain together. Finally, they hoped no other African American women would have to make the same choice about leaving their children behind that they had to make.

A decade after Desert Storm, African American women began to deploy in even greater numbers and for longer periods. Deployment stakes and risks became even higher than during Desert Storm. Combat lines in Operation Iraqi Freedom blurred. Even the rules of military engagement regarding military servicewomen dramatically changed. Every servicewoman was a potential enemy target. Deployed during Operation Iraqi Freedom, African American military mothers had to worry about becoming a POW like Shoshana Johnson, or being shot or kidnapped by insurgents. Like their comrades, they had to worry about roadside improvised explosive devices (IEDs). Like their Desert Storm sisters, they too had to run, hide in shelters, and don gas masks and chemical gear in the sweltering heat. Like those who had served in the desert before them, getting home safely to see their children and grandchildren was a high priority.

Military family researchers rightly contend that deployments are extremely hard on military family members and their children. Researchers are conducting more studies on the issue. A February 2007 American Psychological Association Task Force Report, "The Psychological Needs of the U.S. Military Service Members and their Families," focused on the impact of deployment on military families' mental health. The report contended that deploying "can be a complex and, for some families, overwhelming process."[6]

For children of all ages, the stress of being separated from a military parent can be especially severe. The pain and uncertainty felt by some children of deployed mothers is similar to that experienced by children of divorced parents, the task force noted. Like the three-year-old me, even young children can feel abandoned. They cannot readily articulate their feelings. According to my mother, I frequently had nightmares. On occasion, I would call out "daddy" when I saw men who resembled my dad, much to my mom's embarrassment. Like Hearther's son, small children can get sick. Some even stop eating, and become withdrawn, even after the deployed parent's return. Like the ten-year-old me, today's military children can also feel anxious, worried, and fearful. As I did, they can act out at school or home and not know why they are doing so. They too might want to ask, "When is Mommy coming back home?" Is she in danger? Will she be killed?"

In a 2008 Department of Defense survey of 29,000 military spouses, 60 percent of active duty spouses and 67 percent of reserve-component spouses reported that their children were suffering from increased fear and anxiety. Thirty-six percent of active duty service children and thirty-eight percent of reserve component children showed a decline in grades. Both groups reported that their children exhibiting behavior problems at school. The age groups most negatively affected by deployments are between six and thirteen, followed closely by children ages two to five.[7] Like some of the children of the women interviewed for this chapter, young children of deployed parents can temporarily forget their parents. They will cling to the caregivers who have taken care of them during the deployment.

Deployments are especially hard on military mothers. There are more single moms in the military than fathers, so the stress is a high cost of war. Military women divorce at twice the rate of military men. While they are deployed, many servicewomen report incessant crying and worry about their children's health and safety. Frequently they feel guilt ridden for abandoning their children. Sixty-four percent of servicewomen who have deployed suffer from some type of emotional/mental health problem when they return home.[8]

Added to some of these women's worries is the very real prospect that the children will be left all over again for a redeployment or if their military spouse also has to deploy. Half of married military women are married to military men, making redeployments and joint deployments a danger. The problem is especially acute for African American women, who make up 38 percent of women on active duty. Women generally make up 15 percent of the active duty population. As more African American women enter the armed forces, more will have to deal with the painful choices of leaving one or more children behind.

NOTES

1. U.S. Department of Defense, "Summary of Key Findings from Department of Defense Research," *Report of the Second Quadrennial Quality of Life Review.* (2009), 103. Accessed at http://www.militaryonesource.mil/12038/MOS/Reports/Quadrennial%20Quality%20of%20 Life%20Review%202009.pdf.

2. U.S. Department of Defense, "2011 Demographics: Report of the Military Community" (2012), vi. Accessed at http://www.militaryonesource.mil/12038/MOS/Reports/2011_Demographics_Report.pdf.

3. Michelle Kelley, et al., "Navy Mothers Experiencing and not Experiencing Deployment: Reasons for Staying in or Leaving the Military," *Military Psychology*, 13.1 (2001), 55–71.

4. Christina Jumper, et al., "National Military Family Association Report on the Cycles of Deployment Survey: An Analysis of Survey Responses from April–September, 2005," Nation-

al Military Family Association (2005). Accessed at http://www.militaryfamily.org/assets/pdf/NMFACyclesofDeployment9.pdf.

5. Ramon Hinjosa, Sberna Hinojosa, and Robin Hognas, "Problems With Veteran-Family Communication During Operation Enduring Freedom/Operation Iraqi Freedom Military Deployment," *Military Medicine*, 177.2 (February 2012); 191–197.

6. Shannon J. Johnson, et al., "The Psychological Needs of the U.S. Military Service Members and their Families: A Preliminary Report," report of the American Psychological Association Presidential Task Force on Military Deployment Services for Youth, Families and Service Members (Washington: American Psychological Association, 2007), 16. Accessed at www.apa.org/about/policy/military-deployment-services.pdf.

7. VaJoe.com, "Survey of Military Spouses," survey of the U.S. Department of Defense (2008). Accessed at www.allmilitary.com/board/viewtopic.php?id=24752.

8. Alison Bowen, "Long Tours Extend Heartaches for Military Moms," *WeNews*, an online publication of womensenews.org, (May 27, 2007), 1. Accessed at http://womensenews.org/story/military/070527/long-tours-extend-heartaches-military-moms#.UbJVl9gzXag.

Chapter Five

What Happens in the Desert Stays in the Desert

African American Women Confront Racism and Sexism in the Gulf

Yes, there is rape in the military just as there is in civilian life. There is rape on military bases all over the United States, and also abroad. Being barred from combat jobs hasn't kept it from happening. I spent three weeks in the hands of the "enemy" in Iraq as a prisoner, and I was not raped. Unfortunately many of my fellow female soldiers were raped—sometimes by the very people who were supposed to "have their back..."
—Shoshana Johnson, Prisoner of War, Operation Iraqi Freedom

People are different when they are at war.
—Carolyn Morgan, senior airman, Air National Guard, Operation Desert Storm

Being a black female officer I did not feel that I had the support that the enlisted troops had, nor did I feel like I could talk to the other officers on a personal level. I tried to be mindful of fraternization. I felt extremely isolated. As an officer, we are taught to take care of our people. As Black women, we always take care of others. We sometimes forget to take care of ourselves.
—Gwendolyn Sheppard, Major, U.S. Air Force Reserves, Operation Iraqi Freedom

The first time I heard a spurned U.S. Air Force male fighter pilot snarl the words "Desert Beauty Queen" at the female object of his rejected affection I quickly deduced that the term wasn't exactly complimentary. After hearing military men of all ranks and from all of the services routinely hurl this derisive term at female service members, I ultimately discovered that the mean-spirited moniker meant many things and none of them were nice. To some, a desert beauty queen was the prototypical conniving female gold diggers who slyly took advantage of the driving biological needs of sex deprived servicemen by trading sexual favors for monetary gain. Women would be verbally crowned with this dubious monarchal distinction even if they were deemed so physically unattractive that they (according to some men) wouldn't be able to "buy a date back home" (stateside). If these same "ugly" women had the audacity to spurn men who were "gracious" enough to temporarily lower their standards to have sex with them, they also were dubbed "desert beauty queens." Most crudely put, a desert beauty queen was the proverbial "cockteaser," who refused to fulfill her expected role as combat zone toy/love slut in the testosterone laden highly sexualized male military culture.

Sex play has always been a part of the military's societal makeup. When military people have deployed they have always been expected to work and play hard. Play invariably has involved engaging in sexual liaisons, wanted or unwanted. Whether the serviceman was married back home didn't matter. I had been exposed to the "what happens TDY stays TDY" frat boy mentality from my opening days of military service, so I knew what to expect when I got to Dhahran. In time I learned I would have to subtly and strategically maneuver my way past having to succumb to unwanted sexual overtures while avoiding being put in the untenable position of being crowned a desert beauty queen. Unfortunately, my rank and job position did not always protect me from unwanted attempts to get me to change my mind about my steadfast refusal to engage in these sex play games. Like other women I warily listened to male attempts to cajole and woo me with the predictably old come-on lines, "my wife/girlfriend/fiancée would understand." "We could all die tomorrow, so what's the harm?" or even the most pathetically desperate, "I've been here in this giant sandbox for over a year, and a man has needs."

Some of the men who approached me respected the fact that my religious beliefs prohibited me from engaging in adultery or fornication. Others were not so charitable when they were spurned and retaliated by questioning my sexuality, a dangerous trend in the pre "don't ask, don't tell" era.

To avoid being labeled a cockteaser or a "desert beauty queen," I quickly developed coping and self-protective avoidance strategies. I threw myself into my job, working past my twelve-hour shifts most days. I made sure that I was always in the company of other women or men I deemed safe. I went to nightly church services. I lived with four other female officers, so I also spent evenings in my living area writing letters, watching movies, and reading books. During my four-month deployment, I felt reasonably safe, but I truly resented having to repeatedly explain why "no" really meant no.

I rarely dealt directly with racism during my time in Dhahran, except in dealings with Saudi nationals. By my eleventh year of service in 1991 I had been able to advance well through the ranks and had received great job assignments. I felt that, as long as I did my Air Force job well enough and carried my professional weight, I would be able to compete on the same level as my white male and female counterparts. I took that same military work ethic with me on my desert deployment.

Mindful of the fact that Saudis did not want to work with women, I took advantage of my deep-toned female voice and conducted most of my military business over the telephone to avoid being seen. Most of the host nation men I dealt with over the phone had no idea I was a female. When I did eventually meet a few of them face to face, they were quite surprised that I, a woman, would have so much authority and be able to conduct any type of business on behalf of the United States Air Force. When I absolutely had to go into downtown Dhahran from Khobar Towers,[1] I routinely took my white male technical sergeant with me and let him do all of the talking. It was easier to interact with Saudi officers who had received military training in Great Britain or the United States, but those times were few and far between. Typically I would have tense encounters. At one joint Saudi/American dinner, a Saudi officer of the same rank as me refused to sit next to me. After loudly protesting in Arabic and gesticulating wildly with his arms, motioning for me to leave the room, an American Air Force colonel got up from his seat and traded places with me so I could remain and eat with the other officers. At the time I was not sure if the Saudi officer's histrionics were because I was a female or because I was the only African American in the room. Likely it was both.

It was fortunate that I was able to drive a military vehicle while I was in Dhahran. Since Saudi women are not allowed to drive cars, American service women at the time of my deployment could drive cars only if they wore military uniforms and hats while driving. Personally I was glad we did not have to wear the abaya, the all black, head-to-toe female long sleeved garment with veiled face covering if we went into town. American civilian females who lived there with their families or our female military counterparts assigned to the Saudi Arabian capital, Riyadh, did have to wear abayas. Most American servicewomen did not go into downtown Dhahran by themselves because of the cautionary military orientation briefings received about interacting with the host nation men. We were told not to smile or even look at local male citizens, because they would take a seemingly innocent nonverbal action as an overt sexual invitation. We were also told that Saudis believed that American women were "morally loose women," sexually available. Our charge as servicewomen representing our country was to conduct ourselves to make sure that stereotype vanished.

Rank did not always have its privileges when it came to interacting with Saudi military personnel. Saudi enlisted men would not salute me because I was a woman. They would only salute me if a male was present, no matter if the male was an officer or enlisted. I suppose in their minds they were saluting the male, not me. Determined to uphold the strictest international military protocol, I made sure I saluted every Saudi officer who outranked me. I did not salute those I outranked unless they saluted me first.

During their time in the desert, several of those interviewed for this book had their individual encounters with sexism and racism, relating to host nation men and male soldiers. This chapter outlines how they handled these challenges and the impact these experiences had on their deployments.

MERITOCRACY: THE IDEAL IDEOLOGICAL PATHWAY TO EQUALITY

Since the 1970s the United States military has made great inroads into becoming the premiere organization that models meritocracy and equality. *Meritocracy*,[2] a term first used in 1958, typifies how the military has made a transition to allowing people to advance through ranks and assignments based on their abilities, rather than on their skin color or gender. Tributes are given to the military, even from corporate leaders who are impressed with the military's level of meritocracy. An example is the career of former U.S. Secretary of State Colin Powell, the son of Jamaican working class immigrants. He was given the opportunity to rise to the top military officer ranks. People of color and women continue to routinely join the military because they perceive an equal playing field in job training, in pay, and in the ability to advance professionally.[3]

But there was a long road that had to be traveled to this destination.

In early 1972, Secretary of Defense Melvin Laird addressed Congress in an annual report concerning continual challenges of implementing and sustaining equal opportunity and fair race relations practices while completing the military mission.[4] Secretary Laird's address was uncharacteristically blunt for the times, devoid of the usual doublespeak made when dealing with formidable social issues like race relations:

> Let me candidly tell you that we face formidable problems in the manpower area that are not going to be solved overnight. In addition to complex recruiting and retention problems, we share with the rest of American society the agonizing problems related to race relations. . . . We in the Department of Defense are determined to continue leading the way, as best we can, in seeking solutions to these difficult problems.

Secretary Laird said he had reached these sobering conclusions about the impact of race relations on the Department of Defense's mission after traveling to United States military installations worldwide. He had talked to civilians and service men and women of all ranks to get their views on how to improve equal opportunity in the services. The Department of Defense used ideas gleaned in these conversations to implement significant changes in policy to improve race relations in the services.

One of the most important steps taken was for the military to acknowledge the reality that recruits brought prejudice and hatred to the ranks. To spread the idea of equal rights for everyone, even their fellow soldiers, meant reeducation. In that report to Congress, Laird pragmatically stated, "Education in the dynamics of difference is one of the most important stages the Department of Defense has undertaken. Most people enter military service with insufficient knowledge of, and appreciation for, the culture, history, experiences, and sensitivities of persons of other races to enable them to function well in a multiracial environment."[5]

In 1971, the Department of Defense implemented a new training program, called the Defense Race Relations Institute, at Patrick Air Force Base in Cocoa Beach, Florida. In 1979, the Institute was renamed the Defense Equal Opportunity Institute, (DEOMI), with the "M" standing for *Management*, a word not in the official designation. DEOMI expanded its training objectives beyond racial issues. DEOMI has become the DoD's premiere establishment for providing research, consultation, education, and training. It deals with all human relations relevant topics, including equal opportunity, diversity, cultural competence, and other issues.[6]

DOUBLE THE DEPLOYMENTS: COFIELD SERVES IN DESERT STORM/IRAQI FREEDOM

Jacquelyn Cofield was an African American servicewoman who greatly benefitted from the military's emphasis on advancing equal opportunity. She served twenty-four years in the United States Air Force, mostly in the personnel field. She retired as a senior master sergeant (E-8).

When she was in middle school, Jacquelyn began thinking about serving in the armed forces. In high school, she began to look seriously into joining. "I started looking into the Coast Guard, but I can't swim. Then I saw an ad from the Air Force." When she was out of high school, she met with a U.S Air Force recruiter and was on her way to Lackland Air Force Base in San Antonio, Texas for basic training. On September 8, 1981, she officially became a "blue suiter."

In 1990, Jacquelyn had been in the Air Force almost a decade. She was a staff sergeant assigned to an F-16 Fighter Wing in Torrejon Air Base, Spain, when Operation Desert Shield began. Initially, her wing's leaders thought they would be deployed to Italy to become part of the coalition force there, since they had already undergone many combat exercises in Italy. Instead they were ordered to deploy directly to Qatar.

Upon their arrival, they found that there was neither actual base nor living quarters for them. Instead, the Qatar government put the unit members up in five star hotels. Since there were only three women from Torrejon who deployed and Jacquelyn was the highest ranking of the three, she had a penthouse suite all to herself. The palatial hotel made sure they had free gourmet food available to them at any time. Their life of luxury became short-lived when General H. Norman Schwarzkopf, supreme commander of the International Coalition Forces, was informed about their plush living arrangements. Jacqueline describes his reaction as "livid." Elaborating further she said,

> He called my wing commander and told him that Army troops were living in
> tents. He ordered us to move out of the hotel within twenty-four hours. He said
> if we could not find somewhere to live and if he had to come over there, my
> commander would be on the first thing smoking back to Torrejon.

Since there still were no living quarters facilities built for the troops to reside in, they were forced to move into their work offices and sleep on bare floors until supplies could be sent from Torrejon to construct living spaces. Those stark living conditions were absolutely intolerable, so Jacquelyn and other members of her unit sneaked back to the hotel after six days.

Jacquelyn felt very comfortable doing her job in Qatar. Her primary duty was to manage the Unit Control Center, where she was responsible for personnel accountability and casualty reporting. During Desert Storm, the F-16 wing forces fell into a seamless work regimen. It was almost like being back in Torrejon, she noted. Jacquelyn had been with this F-16 wing for two years by then, and she felt perfectly at ease working with everyone. It was like being part of a family. Membership in a readymade military family gave one certain responsibilities. She was responsible for two younger female airmen who worked with her. She did what she could to realistically allay their fears and keep them productive. "I told them not to be afraid. 'Do your jobs.' They were safe because we knew what we were doing. Besides, when it's your time to go, it's your time to go."

When Operation Desert Storm kicked off at 3 a.m. on January 17, 1991, she was wide awake, standing excitedly on the flight line with others from her unit, waiting for the F16s and other aircraft to take off. She was pumped up with adrenalin and ready to go. For Jacquelyn, the war was finally here. During Desert Storm, four planes were downed, and a couple of pilots briefly became prisoners of war. However, no one in their unit died. SCUD missile attacks were an ever-present danger but the closest one came to her unit was ten miles from the camp. "We had alarms going off around the clock. I never gave it a second thought. This [combat] is what we were trained to do."

WARTIME RACISM AND SEXISM: AFRICAN AMERICAN SERVICE WOMEN'S FIGHT FOR EQUALITY

Several of the interviewees said that they had not experienced overt racism during their deployments. For example Jacquelyn says she did not experience overt racism, although some male maintenance officers did challenge her authority. She admits that this could have been because she was a black female. "They thought the rules did not apply to them. I would talk to them about certain things and they would look at me like 'who are you to talk to me like that?'" One day the command structure was clarified, and they recognized her authority. "I shared office space with the maintenance guys. When the colonel was in, he was in charge. We worked different shifts. One night, as he was leaving, and I was coming in, he said to me, 'Okay, I'm gone. You're in charge.' From that day on I never had any more problems."

While reviewing unit paperwork, she also noticed a potentially racist issue that was affecting the way awards and decorations were being written up for African American and white personnel. "I brought to light what I assumed to be racist practice by members of a maintenance unit that was deployed with the fighter squadron I was assigned to. I was helping the administrative personnel process award packages, and in each case, the black males, though the same rank and position as the white males, were receiving a lesser decoration, if one at all. I immediately discussed it with my commander, who was in charge of the deployed site, and he rectified the situation."

During her service time in Operation Iraqi Freedom in 2003, she experienced something closer to racism. By then she was a senior NCO, a master sergeant (E7), who was originally sent to Jordan to work with a personnel unit of the Connecticut Air National Guard. Everyone in this all-white unit was close-knit like a family. For some reason they treated Jacquelyn like an unwanted step-sibling. No one in the unit liked working with Jacquelyn or appreciated her knowledge about casualty reporting, although she had considerable knowledge about personnel deployment procedures that this unit lacked. "When I got to their unit, they had not set up mortuary affairs, no casualty report status system." Jacqueline knew that these actions were integral components of a Department of Defense personnel program infrastructure that should be set up immediately.

Confident in her ability to do her job well, she continued to try to work within the Guard unit to set up things according to the regulations. She was a senior NCO who ran things by the book. Her insistence on attention to detail and duty frequently set off conflicts with a white male of the same rank as hers. Finally, she asked to be assigned to another unit. One final insensitive incident confirmed her decision to transfer. "When the list for senior master sergeants (E8) was released, I found out that I had a line number for promotion. Neither the commander nor anyone in the Guard unit said anything or even congratulated me. Again, I am not sure if those problems existed because of who I am or because I was trying to ensure that the job was being done correctly."

Upon leaving Jordan, she was assigned to Qatar in a headquarters level job as the superintendent of the Personnel and Manpower Division within the Combined Air Operations Centers (CAOC). Her job responsibilities included ensuring that job codes matched job positions for those forces assigned to the CAOC. It was her job to see that everyone assigned to Southeast Asia was given accurate reporting instructions. She also compiled daily situation reports from all of the deployed sites for the CAOC commander. In this headquarters job, Jacquelyn found her niche and got back into her seamless professional groove.

Jacquelyn credits her spiritual faith with giving her the sound presence of mind to be able to do her jobs during both deployments in the midst of chaotic and dangerous battle zone, without trepidation. "It was amazing during both deployments that I never felt fear. I accredit that to a calming spirit instilled in me by the Lord."

Dealing with racial issues can be a positive experience. Air Force Reservist Major Gwendolyn Sheppard came from a wing with very few African Americans. At the time she served in Operation Iraqi Freedom, she was one of six black officers in a 1400-member Air Reservist Wing. When her civil engineers unit from this organization deployed to Iraq, she was treated to a unique multicultural experience. "The unit we married up with, the 159 Air National Guard Civil Engineer Squadron [from New Orleans, Louisiana], which was half minority. What was so special was seeing so many blacks in supervisory and management positions, including the commander. This was very refreshing, as my home station base was just the opposite."

The challenges of sexism, sexual harassment, and even sexual assault were a lot more pervasive for the interviewees than racism. The combat zone is a military man's work and play ground, where their rules often prevail. Speaking of her experiences in Operation Desert Storm, Captain Reyes said it best: "Males run in packs. Guys will be guys." This testosterone driven mindset did not make serving in combat areas easier for African American women. This flawed principle seemed to describe males even at the highest ranks. Specialist Courtney Salter remembers that her unit had a sergeant major (E9) who was very outspoken and considered cool and down to earth. "I frequently heard him make unnecessary comments to or about females, and I know of things he's done that could have caused a great deal of trouble for him. He and others in leadership positions made light of the adultery within the battalion."

During Patricia Johnson's time in the Gulf, she heard of women being sexual assaulted, and she witnessed women being propositioned by men. "Lots of guys felt like they could do whatever to you, even the married ones. There were guys in our units having affairs, messing around on their wives."

Before Hearther Overstreet's husband arrived to serve with her during Desert Storm, she had several encounters with men that made her feel uncomfortable and uneasy. "The white males thought that being black meant that I was 'easy,' especially since my husband did not arrive at the same time as me. The black males figured I would fool around 'cause my husband would never find out.'" Hearther was no one's desert beauty queen. Staying true to her husband was a high priority for her. "Both sets of males, white and black, got things twisted. Thank God I have the man of my dreams, because the white males ended up respecting me, and a couple of the black males cussed me out, told me that I shouldn't be so uptight. Who the hell did I think I was, anyway? That really surprised me."

Besides being sexually propositioned, Hearther was constantly having her aircraft maintenance technician work skills questioned and tested by her male superiors and peers. "The lack of trust thing really had me going. I was a supervisor, and when me and the guys that worked for me performed repairs, they would fly the aircraft to a more secure site and double check the work. They never did that of the male supervisors and the male workers," she observed.

The danger of actually being sexually assaulted was ever present for Carolyn Morgan. Upon her arrival in Abu Dhabi, the capital of United Arabic Emirates, she was assigned to one of the recreation and relaxation facilities for Desert Shield/Storm troops of all U.S. military forces. At the center, there it was a revolving door of fun, food, and frolicking for scores of men who came into the camp daily from the different combat encampments, tent cities and aircraft flying unit flight lines. The hedonistic "anything goes, for tomorrow we may die," attitude was in full effect at the camp. There were only a few military servicewomen in this desert oasis and those who were assigned there had to be especially careful with their contacts with men, watching out for the most inadvertent nonverbal interaction. "If you made eye contact with any of them, it was considered an invitation," she said. The immense pressure on women to have sex with men included having their reputation be publicly trashed if they resisted. "If you did not give it up to somebody, your name got written on the bathroom walls. That's how high school and childish it was."

In the midst of these potential threats, Carolyn learned early that few of those she initially worked for were concerned about her physical safety.

When she disclosed to a supervisor, an older white, male master sergeant, that she had been raped while in college and was fearful of walking around the encampment by herself, he brushed her off. "He told me that his wife had been raped, and she got over it, and that I had to get over it too," Carolyn said.

One night while she was on duty, her supervisor told her to run a printed message communiqué down to base camp. Carolyn was reluctant to do to this because the message was not an emergency communication. Camp policy was that only urgent/emergency messages were to be transported to the base encampment during late night/early morning hours. Anything nonessential was to be dispatched during the day shift. Her biggest concern was the possibility of being attacked by wild dogs that roamed the camps at night. These dogs were descended from animals left by the Soviets. The dogs were so dangerous that the security police sent out squads at night to them. "I told him I'd be more than happy to run the message down with an escort. You do not send a female down there by herself when the security police are out shooting wild dogs. He got mad." He let her know that she was a woman living in a man's world and that he was in charge. "He told me that I was an airman just like him, and I was in his war, this war with him, and I would do what he told me told, regardless," she remembered. She refused to comply with his order and was reassigned to work in the dining hall.

Carolyn had two bunkmates, both named Ann, while in Abu Dhabi. Her first roommate was raped while she was there, but no one believed her. "They said she was trying to cover up for an affair or a pregnancy or something. All I remember is her crying, crying, and crying in her bunk every day. They finally sent her back to the States." Carolyn and her second roommate inadvertently put themselves in harm's way when they decided to visit a local Moroccan male friend who lived in downtown Qatar. One evening Ann and Carolyn sneaked off base into the city to go to his apartment. While Carolyn admits that sneaking off of the base was not the right thing to do, back then she and Ann did not think it would be a major problem since they trusted this friend. That evening, she recounts, "we ended up sitting around eating, drinking, and Ann and I both passed out. He came in. Ann and I were lying in the same bed. He raped Ann. I was so afraid, I did not breathe. I did nothing. I just freaked. I didn't say anything. She had passed out, and she did not even remember any of it. I told her the next day. She did not believe me."

During Operation Desert Storm, Patricia Johnson managed to keep herself safe from advances of American and other coalition force military males, but two encounters with civilian host nationals left her angry and nervous. During her deployment, she only wanted to be around Americans. She was afraid to go off base because American servicewomen had to be so careful of what they did or said or wore around men. One had to be wary of even the youngest Saudi citizens. "The Saudi kids would pick your pockets or take your watches right off of your wrists."

Sexism in Saudi Arabia was practiced against all women, she noted. Patricia also received the cautionary orientation briefing about Saudis' views of American women. She was offended by their perception that American women are morally deficient, easy sexual prey. Their belief in that stereotype was so complete that they routinely tried to solicit American women for sexual favors, she said. Women were not allowed to go to restaurants by themselves; they had to be accompanied by a man. When the women entered the restaurants to eat, they had to sit in the back of the establishment, accompanied by a male escort. Typically that restaurant segment (called the family section) would be visibly screened or cordoned off from the male section. Once when Patricia was in downtown Dhahran, a Saudi man came up to her and told her that he was glad that she was serving in his country. Thinking that she was going to be congratulated, she briefly looked at him. As part of his so called gesture of gratitude, he grabbed her and kissed her directly in the mouth, frightening her, she said. She also barely escaped being raped by a civilian host nation bus driver. "It was 105 degrees outside, and the bus driver refused to turn on the air conditioner. He stared and started moving close to me and then he started to roam his hands all over my body. He tried to get me to fondle him, but somehow I was able to get away from him and get off of that bus."

Former Captain Coreen Reyes and the women she served with in her unit were not harassed or sexually assaulted. She attributes the fact that she was never propositioned to the way she carried herself. She describes herself as a "no nonsense person." That attitude helped head off any racism or sexism from her superiors or peers during operations Desert Shield/Desert Storm. She agreed that a lower ranking individual would probably find it tougher to fend off advances from men. "A PFC [private first class] does not have the power," she said.

Putting fear in the hearts of would be perpetrators is good strategy for those with protection. Gidgetti Greathouse's ex-husband was serving in Kuwait in the Infantry at the same time she was in the Gulf. "My ex-husband is six foot four inches, 185 pounds, a football player and a body builder. When men found out who my husband was, they left me alone."

Other interviewees developed informal support networks with male and female friends in the deployed area and stateside to help them through the difficulties of dealing with racism and sexism. Some of them also looked to their faith to get them through and keep them protected. However, developing any or all of these strategies does not mean that sexism and racism won't rear their ugly heads against African American women who serve in future military conflicts.

INCIDENTAL SPOILS OF WAR: DECONSTRUCTING THE U.S. MILITARY'S SEXUAL ABUSE CLIMATE

"Man shall be educated for war, and woman for the recreation of the warrior; all else is folly," [7] That misogynistic musing of philosopher Friedrich Nietzsche eerily functions as a gloomy self-fulfilling prophecy of how a sexual abuse climate has managed to develop and thrive in the American military infrastructure. Women have traditionally been considered highly coveted spoils of war for millennia. The raping of a defeated enemy's women and the pillaging of their valuables for battle trophies have been key elements of conquering heroes' rites of passage.

Women who serve side by side with men in the same conquering military institutions today still become incidental spoils of war. On January 25, 2004, two journalists, Miles Moffeit and Amy Herdy from the *Denver Post,* released their report of a seven-month investigation of sexual trauma incidents committed against women during the Operation Iraqi Freedom conflict. They discovered that sexual assaults against service women could be tracked back almost four decades. Women who served in past conflicts participated in surveys that revealed, among other things, that military sexual trauma (MST) was a large, painful part of their service. [8] Nearly 30 percent of 202 female Vietnam War veterans surveyed said they experienced a "sexual encounter" accompanied by force or threat of force, according to the *Congressional Record.* A study of troops in the 1991 Persian Gulf War by Department of Veterans Affairs researchers found that 7 percent of women had reported sexual assaults, and 33 percent had reported sexual harassment. [9]

Prior to 2004, reporting a sexual assault against male counterparts or civilians was just as painful for many victims as the actual physical attack. The reporting process was not private, and intimate details were not kept confidential. Sexual assault complaints weren't always taken seriously or even acted upon when presented to military officials. Some women especially feared making these complaints because they had to be made to, and investigated by, their immediate superior officers, who were usually males and sometimes the actual perpetrators. Unit commanders could decide whether to officially investigate an incident and which punishment to hand out, if any. If a woman decided not to bring the complaint forward, the commander could decide not to pursue the case, even if there was evidence that an assault took place. Women were often not transferred out of the units where they had been assaulted and sometimes still had to face their attackers daily in their work place. Rather than having to submit to cynical "blame the victim" type of investigations conducted by officials (again, usually male) who had no experience in investigating sex related crimes, women chose to remain silent. Some women also kept silent in order to keep a plum assignment or be denied a promotion.

Incredibly, some single women who were raped by married men could be prosecuted under the Uniform Code of Military Justice for committing adultery. At other times, women were denied sexual assault counseling services and not always treated for their physical mental and emotional wounds.

Finally, if the perpetrator was actually charged with a sexual assault and the case made it through the military justice system, the perpetrators were rarely heavily prosecuted and often acquitted. Commanders might even give an administrative punishment, such as taking some pay for a certain amount of time or putting a letter of counseling or reprimand in the offender's permanent record. Some of those who committed the assaults would be allowed to retire from the service with military benefits intact. Their names would not be added to the National Sex Offenders Registry.

In 2003, organizations like the Miles Foundation, a victims' advocacy group, had begun to formally call the military out for not making a concerted effort to prevent military women from being victimized by men in their own units. Sixty members of Congress called for a bipartisan investigation into complaints from women in their districts who reported being sexually assaulted while serving in Iraq and Kuwait. Under pressure, in February 2004, Secretary of Defense Donald Rumsfeld put together a task force to look into how the military dealt with sexual assault allegations.[10] The eight-member task force visited twenty-one military installations and met with 1300 individuals in focus groups. On March 3, 2004, the task force established a Sexual Assault Hotline to allow victims and other individuals to have an opportunity to share their experiences and thoughts.

In April 2004, the task force had finished its work. They presented the following recommendations. The military services should: [11]

- establish a single point of accountability for all sexual assault policy matters within the Department of Defense.
- ensure broadest dissemination of sexual assault information regarding the DoD's policies, programs, and resources available through DoD-wide communication outlets for sexual assault prevention, reporting, response, protection, and accountability.
- develop better operational definitions and delineation of distinctions between terms like sexual harassment, sexual misconduct, and sexual assault, and how those definitions relate to crimes under the Uniform Code of Military Justice.
- establish avenues within DoD to increase privacy and provide confidential disclosure for sexual assault victims.
- establish ways to increase transparency in providing reasons for the handling and disposition of reported sexual assault cases.
- establish an Armed Forces Sexual Assault Advisory Council, composed of key DoD officials and officials of other federal agencies with recognized

expertise in dealing with issues surrounding sexual assault. Such a council would have authority to seek input from other nationally recognized sexual assault experts, as needed.

- develop policies, guidelines, and standards for sexual assault prevention, reporting, response, and accountability.
- encourage reporting through well-established, publicized, and unobstructed reporting channels.
- develop DoD-wide standards and guidelines for sexual assault response to assure that all victims are afforded safety and protection, receive the best care possible, and have a coordinated, timely response, to and resolution of, their cases.
- develop sexual assault "force protection" guidelines for installation and operational use, focused on identification and mitigation of risk factors.
- develop DoD-wide medical standards of care and clinical practice guidelines for treatment and care of victims of sexual assault.
- establish performance metrics for the United States Army Criminal Investigative Lab to ensure more timely forensic evidence processing.
- establish DoD-wide policy requiring victim advocates be provided to victims of sexual assault and create a mechanism for providing victim advocates in deployed environments.
- establish uniform guidelines for commanders' use in responding to victims of sexual assault, including guidelines . . .

  - for assuring that a sexual assault victim's safety and protection needs are met.
  - for positively ensuring a victim's privacy and review the process.
  - for policies regarding how and when reports of sexual assault are forwarded up the chain of command, as well as what information is included in those reports.
  - for addressing a victim's misconduct that occurs in association with a sexual assault.

- ensure that manpower and fiscal resources are authorized and allocated to implement required policies and standards.
- develop an integrated strategy for sexual assault data collection to aid commanders, service providers, legal, staff, and law enforcement in evaluating response effectiveness and system accountability.

In 2006, officials for the Department of Defense were bragging that the agency had made great progress in establishing an effective and robust program.[12]

Even as DoD began to implement these actions, the number of sexual assaults did not subside. In 2008 Department of Defense policy makers still were speaking of their policies as successful.[13] However, in 2008, sexual assaults against military women were termed an epidemic by former U.S. Rep. Jane Harman (D-Calif.). She charged that servicewomen were more likely to be sexually assaulted by men in their own army than they were to be killed by enemy forces. She related that 2947 sexual assaults against women were reported in 2006, 73 percent more than in 2004. In 2007, there were 2688 reports.

The Service Women's Action Network (SWAN),[14] a nonprofit advocacy organization representing women who were active duty or veterans, noted that the spate of sexual assaults had not gotten better in 2011. Nor had the Department of Defense's methods of preventing them, despite the changes it had made to the reporting and tracking system in 2004:

> Despite over twenty-five years of Pentagon studies, task force recommendations and congressional hearings, rape, sexual assault, and sexual harassment continued to occur at alarming rates year after year. In addition to the devastating effects of sexual violence on survivors and their families, rape, sexual assault, and sexual harassment threaten the strength, readiness and morale of the U.S. military, thus effectively undermining U. S. national security.[15]

New York Times reporter Elizabeth Bumiller notes that from 2007 to 2008 there was an 8 percent increase in reported assaults with an 11 percent increase in combat areas. SWAN reports that 3158 military sexual assaults were reported in FY 2010, a decrease from fiscal year 2009. Only about a quarter of these sexual assaults occurred during deployment to a combat zone. In the Pentagon report for 2011, 3192 sexual assaults were reported.[16] However, the 2011 number may be a grossly understate the real situation if 80 to 90 percent of the physical attacks are never reported. The Pentagon estimates that the more accurate estimate of sexual assaults is about 19,000.

A documentary film examining rape in the military served as an eye opening prod for the Department of Defense, just as the *Post* article had in 2004. The 2011 movie, *The Invisible War,* produced by Amy Ziering and directed by Kirby Dick, features the stories of seventy military women, survivors of sexual assault. They candidly tell stories about how they were abused, how they were treated once they reported their abuse, what happened to their abuser, and how their lives had been afterward.

The documentary won the 2011 Sundance Film Festival Audience Award for "Best Documentary."[17] This cinematic exposé of rape and military sexual trauma, with evidence of how few perpetrators were being prosecuted has been lauded for helping change DoD policy regarding sexual assault prevention and training. After reportedly watching the documentary, Secretary of Defense Leon Panetta noted that "sexual assault is a crime that hurts survivors, their families, and the units. In turn, sexual assault reduces overall readiness." The secretary said that he wanted to eradicate a climate of sexual abuse and replace it with a victim advocacy and safety type of climate, in which senior military leadership is held accountable, and perpetrators are vigorously pursued and prosecuted. Since September 2012, under the direction of the secretary, the Department of Defense is now . . .

- elevating disposition authority for the most serious sexual assault offenses.
- working with Congress to establish "special victims unit" capabilities in each of the services, so specially trained investigators and prosecutors can assist when necessary.
- implementing an integrated data system called the Defense Sexual Assault Incident Database for tracking sexual assault reports and managing cases, while protecting victim confidentiality.
- establishing a new policy, giving service members who report a sexual assault an option to quickly transfer from their unit or installation as a way to protect them from possible harassment and to remove them from proximity to the alleged perpetrator.
- establishing a credentialing and certification program aligned with national standards to enhance the quality of support from sexual assault victims' advocates.
- issuing a new policy requiring the retention of sexual assault records for fifty years
- enhancing training for investigators and attorneys in evidence collection, interviewing, and interacting with sexual assault survivors.[18]

A final challenge for the Department of Defense is to remember to protect the most vulnerable from sexual assaults; those who are new to military service, especially those attending basic enlisted and officer training programs. Time will tell whether the protective measures and sexual assault prevention policies will work alongside long standing equal opportunities principles remain in place to mitigate sexual abuse. Perhaps in future conflicts, African American women will no longer have to worry about a dysfunctional military culture that seems to have set in place the axiom, "Whatever happens in the desert, stays in the desert."

NOTES

1. Global Security.Org, "Khobar Towers." Accessed at http://www.globalsecurity.org/military/facility/khobar.htm. Khobar Towers was a housing complex built by the Saudis in 1979 near the city of Dhahran, Eastern Province, Saudi Arabia, but mostly unoccupied until the Gulf War in 1990. During and following the War, coalition forces operating in the Dhahran area occupied the Towers, including service members from the United States, Saudi Arabia, France, and the United Kingdom. Saudi military families currently live in one section. The Towers are primarily high-rise apartment buildings that rise as high as eight stories. The complex also

includes office space and administrative facilities. The perimeter of the U.S., French, and British area is surrounded by a fence and a row of concrete Jersey barriers.

2. *Merriam-Webster Dictionary* defines *meritocracy* as "a system in which the talented are chosen and moved ahead on the basis of their achievement." Merriam-Webster Online Dictionary, (Springfield, MA: Merriam-Webster, Inc., 2013): "Meritocracy." Accessed at http://www.merriam-webster.com/dictionary/meritocracy.

3. *New World Encyclopedia* contributors, "Colin Powell," *New World Encyclopedia. Accessed at* http://www.newworldencyclopedia.org/p/index.php?title=Colin_Powell&oldid=959041 (accessed May 30, 2013).

4. Melvin R. Laird, "Equal Opportunity and Race Relations in the Department of Defense." *Commander's Digest*, 12.2 (18 May 1972): 1–2.

5. Ibid.

6. Bryan Ripple, "DEOMI's New Commandant Personifies Diversity," on Patrick Air Force Base, Brevard County, Florida, Website. Accessed 15 June, 1912 (updated 6/20/2012) at http://www.patrick.af.mil/news/story.asp?id=123306719.

7. Nietzsche's misogynistic views are infamous, though some readers say that this and some other comments have been taken out of context. See, for example, Cheri Block Sabraw, "Nietzsche out of Context,"in Sabraw's blog, *Notes from Around the Block* (24 July 2009). Accessed at http://cheriblocksabraw.com/2009/07/24/nietzsche-out-of-context/.

8. U.S. Department of Veterans Affairs, National Center for PTSD, "Military Sexual Assault," 1 January 2007. Accessed at http://www.ptsd.va.gov/public/pages/military-sexual-trauma-general.asp.

9. Miles Moffeit and Amy Herdy, "Female GIs Report Rapes in Iraq War: 37 Seek Aid After Alleging Sex Assaults by U.S. Soldiers," *Denver Post*, 1/25/2004 (updated 5/18/2005). Accessed at http://www.denverpost.com/search/ci_0001913069.

10. Ellen Embrey, et al., "Task Force Report on Care for Victims of Sexual Assault," U.S. Department of Defense, April, 2004: 7. Accessed at http://www.defense.gov/news/May2004/d20040513SATFReport.pdf.

11. Ibid., 11–14.

12. U.S. Department of Defense, "Department of Defense Report on Military Services Sexual Assault for CY 2006," March 15, 2007, 4. Accessed at http://www.sapr.mil/media/pdf/reports/2006-annual-report.pdf.

13. U.S. Department of Defense, "Department of Defense FY07 Report on Sexual Assault in the Military," March 15, 2008: 26. The entire report is self-congratulatory in its description of new or improved programs and outreach efforts. Accessed at http://www.ncdsv.org/images/DoD_Annual_Report_on_Sexual_Assault_in_the_Military-FY2007_3-2008.pdf.

14. For more information on the Service Women's Action Network, see the organization Website at http://servicewomen.org/.

15. Service Women's Action Network, "Quick Facts: Rape, Sexual Assault and Sexual Harassment in the Military," July 2012. Accessed at http://servicewomen.org/wp-content/uploads/2012/10/Final-RSASH-10.8.2012.pdf.

16. U.S. Department of Defense, "Department of Defense Annual Report on Sexual Assault in the Military: Fiscal Year 2011," April 2012, p. 33. Accessed at http://www.sapr.mil/media/pdf/reports/Department_of_Defense_Fiscal_Year_2011_Annual_Report_on_Sexual_   Assault_in_the_Military.pdf.

17. Sundance Film Festival Archives, "Invisible War." Accessed at http://history.sundance.org/films/7128 The Invisible War

18. U.S. Department of Defense, "Initiatives to Combat Sexual Assault in the Military," n.d. Accessed at http://www.defense.gov/home/features/department_messages/DoD_Initiatives_to_Combat_Sexual_Assault.pdf.

Chapter Six

Where My Health Comes From

*African American Servicewomen
Battle Gulf War Illnesses*

I was actually told it was all in my head and that I was going to be charged with malingering because I had gone to the doctor so much.
—Carolyn Morgan, Operation Desert Storm

In the beginning, we had makeshift latrines (and during convoy no latrines at all), and they were not in the best of conditions in reference to cleanliness and stability. I had to learn to be okay with the risk of being seen, I had to learn to "go now and breathe later," and unfortunately I taught myself to wait until I could hold it no longer, so that I would spend as little time as possible in the box or at the hole.
—Courtney Salter, Operation Iraqi Freedom

Each time I deployed my hair began to fall out. Other than that, I was mentally, emotionally, physically fine.
—Jacquelyn Cofield, Operation Desert Storm, Operation Iraqi Freedom

It seems important to look at the health sacrifices given by African American women during and after the Gulf wars, although the afflictions equally affected men and women soldiers of all races. A few of the interviewees fortunately did not suffer any lasting problems or ill health effects from their experiences in the Gulf. Some however did and are still dealing with these illnesses. In a few cases they are still battling the government to get the help and medical compensation they desperately need and rightfully earned. The subject is a sensitive one to me, as I am among those whose deployment led to mysterious and debilitating illness.

This chapter will outline how some of these African American military women have sacrificed their health while serving this country.

Two dramatic environmental adjustments jolted me from mind numbing jetlag as I disembarked from a military passenger plane in Dhahran, Saudi Arabia, in August 1991. First, my body sagged as I wilted in the 125-degree furnace blast of acrid smoky air enveloping the concrete tarmac. Then my eyes started tearing up and tingling; my throat burned as if I had swallowed hot coals. Caught up in a frenzied fit of coughing and gagging, I could barely catch my breath.

I was not the only Operation Desert Storm new arrival experiencing this respiratory agony that day, nor would this be the last time I would endure these symptoms during my deployment. I eventually discovered that the trigger for my coughing jags was oil well fire smoke. Six hundred Kuwait oil wells ignited by fleeing Iraqi troops in February 1991 were still burning in August when I arrived. Thick plumes of smoke managed to make their way into Saudi Arabia until I returned stateside that November. On November 6, 1991, firefighters extinguished the last oil well fire.

The nagging, hacking cough and soreness of throat continued for several months after my deployment. Since then I have had chronic bronchitis, sinusitis, pleurisy (an infection of the lining of my left lung) and other serious respiratory conditions. Other health problems also cropped up without obvious cause. I was in good health when I went to Saudi Arabia. I visited the doctor once while I was deployed. I even tried to stay in shape by exercising in the Khobar Towers living area gym whenever I had the chance. Upon my return stateside, however, it became increasingly difficult for me to exercise consistently. My muscles and joints were in chronic pain. I found it more difficult to run or walk fast. My energy level was low; I suffered bouts of recurring chronic fatigue that became more and more pronounced. My sleeping patterns became increasingly erratic. I could sleep for hours and still not feel refreshed when I began my day. I initially attributed these health challenges and physiological changes to the high stress and nonstop demands of my job. In hindsight, I probably should have taken a short vacation, gotten a post-deployment medical checkup, and rested my jet-lagged mind and body, but I didn't.

Fiercely dedicated to duty, I went back to work immediately upon returning from Saudi Arabia. The completion of my base's new mission was paramount, albeit final. Eaker Air Force Base was going through a very painful base closure process. Ensuring that our Public Affairs Division maintained a strong, comprehensive publicity operation regarding the complexities of this closure caused my staff and I to work long hours.

I also hated making appointments with military doctors because of the fear that going to see them too often would show up on my military record when I was looked at for future assignments. No one in the military wants to be tagged as a malingerer, especially a senior captain with a promotion line number to major. I hoped to seamlessly transition into the field grade officer ranks before retirement. I failed to look into what was happening to my health. Instead, I decided to fix myself without conventional medical intervention. I began my own holistic health regimen. I changed my diet, took more vitamin supplements, and increased my exercise routines. Still, my health problems continued and grew worse, even after my retirement on July 1, 1995.

Eleven years later, my chronic muscle and joint pain had become absolutely unbearable. Mental fatigue made me feel as if I was living in a perpetual fog. I told my increasingly concerned family and friends that I felt as if I was spending my days wading through giant vats of gelatin.

Frustrated, I finally decided that I would have to put my trust and overall health in the hands of my general family practice doctor, Sandra Bohnstengel. This turned out to be a good health move for me. Dr. Bohnstengel sent me to an orthopedic specialist. He, in turn, sent me to a local rheumatologist who made a series of tests. Finally I had a diagnosis for the painful maladies that had been plaguing me since 1991. I had fibromyalgia.[1]

I was relieved yet puzzled about that diagnosis. Looking back through my family's medical history, I could find no one on either side of my family who had claimed this as a familial health issue. When I started investigating my own health timeline, I looked back to when I began having symptoms of fibromyalgia and recurring respiratory problems that also had to be treated. Since I was healthy before I went to Saudi Arabia in 1991 and only began to have pain and fatigue after I came back from the Gulf, I began to wonder if deploying there had exposed me to something that adversely affected my body.

Eventually, after conducting my own empirical research about fibromyalgia and respiratory problems, I encountered other veterans who had come back from the Gulf with similar symptoms. I learned that I was not alone in asserting that my health problems were tied to deploying to the Gulf in support of Operation Desert Storm in 1991.

Hundreds of service members returned to the United States after Operation Desert Storm experiencing a host of unexplained illnesses and debilitating health problems. These illnesses included individual symptoms such as headaches, memory loss, skin lesions, rashes, fatigue, muscle and joint pain, and gastrointestinal disorders. They had such chronic multi-symptom illnesses as fibromyalgia (FMS), chronic fatigue syndrome (CFS), and multiple chemical sensitivity (MCS). Others noted an increase of psychiatric illnesses, posttraumatic stress disorder (PTSD), and depression. Some male veterans complained of "burning semen." Service members of both genders and their spouses reported birth defects in children born after the veteran's return from the Gulf. The media quickly dubbed this medical phenomenon Gulf War syndrome.[2] At first the military, medical, and even some preliminary scientific research consensus was that these illnesses (if they did actually exist) were primarily the outgrowth of rapid deployment/combat related stressors. Gulf War syndrome was also viewed by some in the medical field and in government as a psychological illness.

Thomas Shriver, Amy Miller, and Sherry Cable explained in *Sociological Quarterly*, "Government agents and medical personnel have routinely attributed the symptoms to psychiatric conditions. This dismissal deeply angered veterans, women perhaps more less so than men because women's ailments are so frequently diagnosed as psychological."[3] For several years after the war, the U.S. government's unwavering position rested on the contention that there was not enough conclusive data to prove the existence of a scientific correlation between veteran illnesses and the risks posed in the Gulf War.

Through the efforts of fifty grass roots organizations, Gulf War veterans mounted a fierce battle on the home front, calling on all levels of government to formally recognize what came to be known as "Gulf War Illness" and provide needed treatment and compensation for affected service persons and their families.

To some veterans and active duty service members, the refusal to acknowledge Gulf War illness was eerily reminiscent of a similar denial regarding exposure to agent orange. In the Vietnam War, from 1962 to 1971, a mix of herbicides called Agent Orange was sprayed by the U.S. military to kill foliage that camouflaged enemy shelters and hideouts. Exposure had a grave impact on the health of Vietnam veterans and their families. Finally the government was forced to change its position about agent orange after years of medical studies proved that exposure to it and other herbicides used during that military conflict caused cancer and other health problems.[4] Gulf veterans and their advocates lobbied hard to avoid repeating that history. Currently one in four veterans of the 1991 conflict suffer from Gulf War illness.

In 1998, with many questions still unanswered, Congress enacted PL 105-277, the Persian War Gulf Veterans Act, and PL 105-368, the Veterans Enhancement Act. The measures established an independent panel of scientists and veterans to review all federal research studies and programs conducted about Gulf War veterans' health.[5] After a comprehensive empirical review in November 2008, the Department of Veterans Affairs was forced to acknowledge that the right questions about the mysterious maladies that Gulf War veterans had suffered since 1991 were finally answered. The **Research** Advisory Committee on Gulf War Veterans' Illnesses handed the veterans a victory in the battle for recognition, noting:

> There is no question that Gulf War illness is a real condition with real causes and serious consequences for affected veterans. Study after study has consistently documented this multisymptom condition in large numbers of Gulf War

veterans. Research has also shown that this pattern of illness does not occur after every war and cannot be solely attributed to psychological stressors during the Gulf War. Because research studies have so compellingly demonstrated that Gulf War illness cannot be explained simply as the expected result of wartime stress, it remains the responsibility of the federal government to fully elaborate the source and nature of this condition, to care for affected veterans, and to prevent similar problems from happening in the future.[6]

In 2010, the Committee on Gulf War and Health came up with yet another new name for the malady—chronic multi-symptom illness (CMI). Veterans who have CMI often have physical symptoms such as fatigue, joint and muscle pain and gastrointestinal symptoms and cognitive symptoms such as memory difficulties. Individuals may also have multiple unrelated illnesses with shared symptoms such as CFS, FMS, and irritable bowel syndrome.[7] The name change signified the inability to determine the origin of these numerous illnesses the veterans were suffering from and the difficulty of treating them.

Even with the new name, the government did not set aside its reticence toward accepting responsibility and impatience with disagreeable researchers. Funding support previously given to researchers on CMI was curtailed. The government did not concur with a 2009 study's finding that "neurotoxins such as anti-nerve agent pills, insect repellent and the nerve agent sarin caused neurological changes to the brain and these changes seemed to correlate with different Gulf illness symptoms."[8] The government claims that the study was a waste of funding and was fraudulent in its findings. Dr. Robert Haley, a preeminent scholar who studies CMI, wrote the disputed 2009 study report. He is chief of epidemiology at the University of Texas Southwestern Medical Center in Dallas, yet he received a substantial cut in government funding because of these findings. Undaunted, he worked with fifteen other researchers on their own time, using alternative sources of funding to conduct another large scale study. This study found evidence that CMI is due to damage to the autonomic nervous system.[9]

According to their research findings, affected veterans fall into three categories: Syndrome 1: cognitive and depression problems; Syndrome 2: confusion, and ataxia, which is similar to early Alzheimer's disease; Syndrome 3: severe body pain. CMI could also be a combination of all of the syndromes. There are still unanswered questions about CMI. According to Dr. Haley, "the disease itself is so difficult to express and to understand . . . doctors don't know what the disease is, but if you can't figure out what the disease is, the other problems will not fall in line."[10]

Adding more credibility to Dr. Haley's findings, in January 2013 the Institute of Medicine revealed that some veterans who fought in Operation Iraqi Freedom and the current Afghanistan conflicts are also suffering from CMI. That new empirical revelation could now force the government to expand its geographical definition and timeline regarding CMI. Specifically veterans who served in these last two conflicts can also qualify for Gulf War benefits associated with the disease. There is still no consensus among physicians, researchers, and others, however, as to what has caused the illness. According to a report in *Army Times*, "There is a growing belief that no specific casual factor or agent will be identified."[11]

TAKING BIRD BATHS AND USING LATRINES: AFRICAN AMERICAN WOMEN FIGHT FILTH IN THE DESERT

Cleanliness in a combat area has always been an essential part of maintaining mission readiness and health on the battlefield. Nurse Florence Nightingale was one of the first health advocates who strongly promoted personal and institutional hygiene for troops. Today, far more advanced life saving hygiene practices focus on a service member's body and also their combat area living quarters and work areas. Historically, academic studies that examined the importance of developing and maintaining hygiene standards in combat arenas primarily focused on males. Now that women are deploying to combat areas, there are some recent studies on women service members.

Sanitation is identified as one of the biggest environmental challenges affecting women's health, as well as men's, in the Gulf wars. One Institute of Medicine report outlined how troops often fought a losing battle in maintaining hygienic conditions in combat zones: "Sanitation was often primitive, with strains on latrines and communal washing facilities. Hot showers were infrequent, the interval between laundering uniforms was sometimes long and desert flies were a constant nuisance."[12] Sharon Cohen noted that hygiene issues especially have had an impact on the health of women who served in Iraq and Afghanistan conflicts. "Some of the short-term health problems are likely tied to the harsh realities of war, where women can go weeks without a shower and spend months hauling gear and lifting heavy weapons in triple digit heat."[13]

The interviewees for this book noted the importance and difficulties of keeping good hygiene in their encampments. Kim Hatcher says she frequently washed her clothes out by hand to keep them clean. Gidgetti Greathouse said she never felt dirt free while dealing with the blowing sand and long lines for the bathrooms during Operation Desert Storm. "I never felt clean and could not get clean enough. I would save my drinking water to take a bird bath at night. I never took being clean for granted again." Her bathroom habits also changed drastically, partly because of her abject fear of the constant SCUD missile attacks and partly from having to deal with the filthiness of the latrines. "I got so I would not go to the bathroom. I did not void until the last SCUD attack. I could go a month without going to the bathroom," she said.

Courtney Salter experienced infrequent showers and long lines to foul smelling latrines, sometimes overflowing with feces and urine, during Operation Iraqi Freedom:

> Physically I think I am unhealthier as a result of habits I learned while deployed. In the beginning we had makeshift latrines (and during convoys, no latrines at all) and they were not in the best of conditions (in reference to cleanliness and stability). I had to learn to be okay with the risk of being seen, I had to learn to go now and breathe later and unfortunately I taught myself to wait until I could hold it no longer, so that way I would spend as little time as possible in the box or at the hole.

Courtney's reluctance to use the latrines also had to do with their location. The dining area was near what soldiers in Courtney's unit called a "piss ditch," a crude euphemism for the hole in the ground latrines. "I stopped eating. People got sick, vomiting, diarrhea with something we called ATM (ass to mouth). It got overwhelming because people were not washing their hands," she said.

During the Iraqi conflict, Major Gwendolyn Sheppard and other members of her encampment also contracted a virus that featured a sore throat and nagging cough. She said she had the cough the entire time she was deployed, and it lasted at least five months after she returned to the states. The virus left her with a partially paralyzed larynx. Gwendolyn wonders if a waste removal process that nearby units used had might have had an impact on her health. "The Army was burning everything around us 24/7. I have no idea what they were burning. I do know they were burning the trash. I also know they were burning waste materials. We were surrounded by Army units on all four sides. No matter which way the wind blew, we were getting it." This daily practice of burning trash and waste was likely carried over from Desert Storm. Ironically, one of Patricia Johnson's deployment duties as a lower enlisted ranked soldier was to help burn her unit's waste each day with kerosene. One reason veterans have suffered from chronic pulmonary disorders could be that they were burning almost 240 tons in open pits as well as having to breathe in dust and sand full of bacteria and heavy medals.[14]

For some of those I interviewed, skin rashes were a problem. Patricia Johnson said she had horrible skin rashes. Jacqueline Cofield also had skin rashes during both of her deployments but confesses that she most likely had skin problems because she "does not do heat well." Since her time in Desert Storm, Hearther Overstreet said, she still has "some type of skin disorder that just won't quit."

Not only did several of interviewees get sick during deployment, but they faced the prospect of bringing some disorder or sickness back home that could be transmitted to their families. This was a real threat. When both Gidgetti and her ex-husband returned from Desert Storm, they had a baby daughter who was born healthy but began to have health problems shortly after birth. "We had a daughter and at first she was fine. Then she started having problems, sleep seizures, extra problems with her heart. We had to have her on a heart monitor for awhile. Both of us wondered if that [deployment to the Gulf] contributed to her illness." Gidgetti also came back from the Gulf with a mysterious malady that caused the Army to put her on what is called a profile three (P-3) duty restriction. This can be given after a medical evaluation determines whether a solider is fit for active duty and can continue to work in that soldier's specialty. [15] "I went from a size seven ring finger to a size thirteen. I started having problems with my bones."

BEATING BACK BALDNESS IN THE GULF: BLACK FEMALES FACE HAIR PRESERVATION CHALLENGES

Keeping one's hair groomed and styled in accordance with military regulations also proved to be a challenge for many African American women who deployed during both conflicts. Gwendolyn said she kept her hair cropped short so she would not have to worry about trying to maintain complicated hair styles without the proper ethnic hair products.

Several interviewees said they experienced hair thinning, breakage, even significant loss. Jacquelyn said she had hair loss in during both conflicts. Gidgetti lost some of her hair while deployed and still has hair problems that she says she did not have prior to the Gulf wars. "My hair will only grow to a certain length and then it will break off," she says. More fortunate was Carolyn Morgan, who says she was able to save her hair and keep it successfully groomed partly because the African American women in her encampment shared hair products and did each other's hair. Several interviewees said they owed their hair preservation to thoughtful family members who sent African American hair relaxer products. Courtney, however, remembers that trying to maintain her hair was one of the most stressful aspects of her deployment.

> With all of the dust storms, hard water, and limited resources for African American females, I had a lot of breakage, shedding and damage in general. I know it seems minor and superficial, but there was a noticeable difference (other than race) in Caucasian females and African American females. It was easy for them [the Caucasian females] to go into the PX and purchase whatever shampoo was available, wash their hair, and you would never know what damage, if any, that they had. We on the other hand cannot use just any kind of hair product. And for those with relaxed hair, unless there was a faithful supporter stateside who sent relaxers regularly, we were out of luck.

LIVING IN THE SHADOW OF FEAR: AFRICAN AMERICAN
SERVICEWOMEN AND PTSD

Several empirical studies conducted since the 1990s show that those who deployed to the Gulf were two to three times more likely to suffer from PTSD later than those who were not deployed. Since the beginning of the Iraq conflict, 26,000 female veterans have been diagnosed with PTSD. More experienced Military Sexual Trauma (MST) from sexual assaults. Women who served in Operation Desert Storm also suffered from PTSD, but they were less likely to report problems and seek treatment. For women who served in either Iraq or Afghanistan, MST was as likely as actual combat to lead to PTSD.[16] Being in the midst of a dangerous war zone by its nature causes service members to constantly worry about family and friends, wondering whether they will be alive to see them again. Women taking part in convoy travel are exposed to dangers of being captured, blown up by IEDs (improvised explosive devices), or shot by insurgents. Women in insurgency roles must deal directly with Iraqi and Afghan women since American men are not allowed to have physical or social contact under Muslim law. This is a stressful assignment since insurgent Iraqi women and children may be armed with bombs and other weapons, desiring to kill coalition forces of either gender.

PTSD can be brought on by the mere threat of an attack. When the warning alarm for a possible or imminent attack sounded, all of the interviewees mentioned having to go into Mission Oriented Protective Posture 4 (MOPP 4).

MOPP 4 was especially stressful and scary for Gidgetti. The first time an alarm for a SCUD missile attack sounded and her unit went into MOPP 4 status she knew she had to act quickly and correctly don and seal the gas mask, and put on the protective hood, long gloves, foot wear covers and a protective cover over her uniform.[17] Patricia Johnson remembers being frequently "stressed out and very tense" during hours in MOPP 4 chemical gear in 115-degree heat, Likewise, Maria Quillan relates that her most stressful times during Operation Iraqi Freedom deployment was constantly "getting into my gas mask, and chemical suit and running to the nearest shelter, praying and waiting for the 'all-clear' alarm signal." She was exposed to the MOPP 4 alarms from her first day in Kuwait. MOPP 4s often came during the night she said. "I was always the first one up in my tent. It seemed like the younger women could sleep through the alarms." She would be wide awake and very afraid. On one particular day, alarms went off several times, twice when she was in a shower and once as she was in the latrine.

The alarms and protection perimeter around their camp did not make Maria feel safe at all. She never knew whether that particular day would be her last on earth. "I did feel I was in danger. I saw the Patriot missiles, and they were all around. We had to have our wills made when we were activated. You actually feel that you may die. I had never felt that before. It was serious and I wrote that in my journal and I said I did not want to have a gun in my hand—give me a spoon," she said.

Besides her fears, the fifty-five-year-old naval reservist had a host of health problems. Maria was on medical restriction and had dangerously high blood pressure. Inexplicably, the Navy still cleared her to deploy with her unit to Kuwait in January 2003. The decision baffled the military medical staff in Kuwait who had to treat her aggravated illnesses. "The doctors there wanted to know why I was sent there," she said. Of course, the doctors in Kuwait never considered sending her home. At the end of her deployment, the impending exodus from Kuwait did not improve her health or allay her fears. Her unit's departure was anything but smooth. The return home was very stressful. "It was in the middle of the night, and it was nerve wracking. We spent a long time waiting. I wanted to see trees, see green; I wanted to hear motors and generators. But I was comfortable with quiet."

Maria's Gulf war experience left her nerves so frayed that she is still under a Veterans Administration doctor's care in Roanoke, Virginia, a decade later. Besides her other ailments, she has PTSD. She is receiving 100 percent service illness disability. As far as she is concerned, since the Navy sent her without considering her health, this payment is the very least they can do. "They're simply paying me for the mistake they made," she said.

PTSD COUNSELING FOR ALL VETERANS: AFRICAN AMERICAN WOMEN FACE THEIR FEARS IN THERAPY

Felecia Weston readily admits that she has survivor's guilt. Every day she tells herself that she is not supposed to be alive. On February 25, 1991, she was wounded during Desert Storm when SCUD missile debris hit her encampment. Thoughts of that day haunt her. "It has been so many years, but I still feel guilty for being here." This guilt has gotten so entrenched inside of her that it has affected her attempts to have and sustain intimate relationships. "I feel so guilty for being here that whenever a man starts to get close to me, I wouldn't dare let someone say 'I love you' because I don't feel I'm worthy of that because nobody knows my secret. I have lived through this and I shouldn't have. I will do something mean to them to try to run them off. I have been doing this for years. I will push him away. I'm not entitled to love, I have to live alone. I have my mother and my sister."

A decade after her injury, the horrors of 9/11 plunged her further into PTSD. When Felicia saw the plane crash into the first New York City World Trade Center building, she first thought it was an isolated incident. Once she learned that this was a terrorist attack, she says, she "had a meltdown. . . . As soon as I found out what it was, I had a severe anxiety attack. It sent me right back to Dhahran."

Over the past few years, she has been treated by a doctor twice a week at a local Veterans Affairs hospital. She describes him as a God send in her life. "If it hadn't been for him I would be dead. He's like a rock; he always gives me positive feedback," she says. Her doctor saw her through a significant part of her emotional healing therapy process after she learned that she could not have children. Her battle scars also continue to affect her optically. Because of her eye wounds, she must wear glasses. She suffers from incapacitating headaches.

After Patricia Johnson's harrowing experience in the Gulf she had to confront the fact that she had PTSD. To confront the inner turmoil, she decided to go into therapy and talk to other veterans who had the same experience. "My group was about twenty-five people. I was the only Desert Storm person. Most were Vietnam veterans," she said.

Patricia said she was especially touched by an African American male Vietnam veteran's story. He served in military in the 1960s when the U.S. was in the midst of a social civil war. African Americans were still waging a battle in the nation for equality. Black guys were fighting two wars, he told the group. These soldiers had to battle both the North Vietnamese and the whites who were discriminating against them. Some wanted him to have no rights. This could be more than a war of words. "He had to sleep with his weapon because he did not know who would use theirs against him."

An Operation Desert Storm veteran, Carolyn's PTSD was triggered by the news reports coming out of Operation Iraqi Freedom. She already was suffering from other Gulf War service generated illnesses. Carolyn was operated on to repair a hernia when she was in the Gulf. The surgeons unintentionally cut a major nerve in her groin. She was in a lot of pain afterwards, but was still was declared medically fit to do her recruiting duties. "I was always having this leg pain and I was always going to the doctor." She experienced other health problems as well.

Back home in Wisconsin, Carolyn went to a Veterans Affairs Department hospital physician. After conducting a series of medical tests, the VA physician found sarcoidosis, a severe lung inflammation disease. The doctors could not determine its origin, but they knew it was related to hazardous chemicals. Carolyn believes her Desert Storm duties in Abu Dhabi probably exposed her to quite a bit of chemicals. Daily she cleaned the tents of the troops who came from encampments near the oil fields or locations where waste and other hazardous materials were burned. "I could have gotten it from what they had bought in from those areas," she relates.

At first, no one believed Carolyn was sick. Supervisors thought she was using imaginary illnesses to keep from doing her duties. "I was initially told that it was in my head and I would be charged with malingering because I was going to the doctor so much. They were telling me I wasn't really sick yet my white blood count was elevated. They weren't even listening to me about my pain." Only after the doctor in Wisconsin provided the right diagnosis was she vindicated.

Another medical problem arose when she was put on prednisone to treat the lung infection; she gained sixty pounds. This rapid weight gain affected her ability to do her Air Force recruiter duties. She could not fit into her military uniform. "How can you be a recruiter if you cannot wear your uniform?"

In desperation, Carolyn tried to get a medical discharge from her Air National Guard unit, but Guard medical officials kept clearing her. So did active duty officers when she went to them. Finally she was released from the National Guard as an "overage," part of the U.S. military reduction of service member numbers after Operation Desert Storm.

Medically, physically, and emotionally damaged, she hopped from job to job. She went on unemployabilty status through the VA. "I did not work for four years," she said. She got VA compensation for her lung problem and also later for PTSD. "I got my PTSD when the Iraqi War kicked in. I started to have the feelings of doubt, like I did not complete my job; I had these feelings of failure. We did not do exactly what we were sent over there to do, so a lot of that stuff started coming back."

While Gidgetti does not describe her symptoms as PTSD; she readily confesses that she went to the VA to talk to others who could help her to find herself. In 2000 she started meeting with other vets. Eventually she was able to help herself refocus through these lifesaving conversations with vets. She found that she needed to have a sense of camaraderie, to talk to people who had been through what she had been through in a combat zone. She was not the same young woman when she returned home from her deployment, and to her it was obvious that it changed dynamics of relationships with friends and family members. "I got out of the military not knowing what to do. My family did not understand. My ex-husband did not understand me. My behavior was different, I looked different. When I came back, I was lost; I did not know what to do. There was no one, day to day, telling me to do things. I found myself getting these odds and ends jobs that did not work out."

Because of stories like those of Carolyn, Patricia, Maria, and other African American female veterans, the VA's National Center for PTSD continues to collaborate with leading trauma specialists, researchers, and clinicians. The goal is to develop more effective therapeutic programs and provide up-to-date information on efforts to combat the residual emotional, mental, and even physical pain that PTSD/MST can bring to women. But for some female veterans this new-found focus on PTSD and MST is long overdue and is not nearly enough. In the twenty-first century, the Department of

Defense and the VA still need to do even more to properly provide quality medical care for all aspects of female veterans' health.

FOR THE HEALTH OF IT: VA AND DOD HEALTH PROGRAMS HELD ACCOUNTABLE

Gwendolyn Sheppard charges that the military did not take very good care of the health of reservists who deployed to the Gulf when they came back home. When people came back from the Gulf, she noted, they were supposed to get a Post Deployment Health Assessment. "They are supposed to look at it and see if you have any additional needs," she explained. She made sure that members of her unit who needed extra medical attention had hospital appointments at the Naval Station Great Lakes, a large naval base near Chicago. She expected that, after being given thorough examinations and upon discovery of health problems, her people would enter the military's medical system. She assumed that their health issues would be dealt with until they could be properly treated.

However, the naval hospital did not automatically make follow up appointments, even for or those who needed them. Gwendolyn took on the logistical challenge getting her people back and forth to the hospital, so they could be properly cared for. Some still fell through the administrative cracks and missed out on the care they needed. The state of her own health when she came back from the Gulf was not good. "I had a lot of memory loss. I found out that I had Gulf War illness." She is still being treated but said the military could have done a far better job of taking care of her health and the health of those reservists who deployed with her.

For some of the interviewees who have left the military, the Department of Veterans Affairs is where their mental and physical health must first be addressed. However the VA readily admits that it has not always met the needs of its female veterans. Approximately 1.8 million women have served in the U.S. military. The VA admits that it is not effective enough in serving the 8 percent of the current veteran population who are females. In ten years, VA statisticians foresee, women will make up 16 percent of the veteran population.

At this writing, the current Veterans Affairs secretary is Eric K. Shinseki. He believes that VA doctors who treat veteran women have not, in the past, kept up on medical problems specific to women, such as reproduction issues, sexual trauma, eating disorders, and menopause. Until recently, some VA centers did not even have separate bathrooms or waiting rooms for women. Women returning from the Gulf and Afghanistan wars have been reluctant to go to VA clinics because of the impression that clinic care is adequate only for male veteran medical needs. To combat that perception, the VA now has full-time care managers for women at all 144 veteran health care clinics and hospitals. The VA also offers advanced training for its health care providers on women's health issues. More female practitioners are on staff. Over half of the counselors and therapists for the VA are women. The VA hopes that, by actively changing its historically all-male culture and advancing its awareness of women veterans' needs, more female veterans will go to the centers for their physical and mental health needs.

Serving active duty and retired members, the DoD or Military Health System is one of the largest health systems in the nation. In 2012 the U.S. Government Accountability Office (GAO) was tasked by the National Defense Authorization Act for Fiscal Year 2012 with reviewing the female specific health care services provided by the Department of Defense. The report lauded DoD for providing more thorough redeployment screenings of women for pregnancy and other illnesses that could prevent them from deploying. It also lauded DoD for making sure that female health specific issues could be addressed better in the combat arena. Some of the female service members cited in the report raised concerns about being able to get certain types of medication, for example means of birth control, while deployed.[18]

Recent news reports show that sexual violence against women remains a major military issue. An anonymous survey reported as many as 26,000 assaults in 2012, up from 19,000 in 2011. DOD has taken steps to prevent sexual assault and to treat women who have been sexually assaulted, but obviously more needs to be done to educate first responders and health providers on how to properly treat and assist a female service member with physical or mental needs. The GAO report concludes, "DoD has taken steps to meet the health needs of deployed servicewomen but actions are needed to enhance care for sexual assault victims." The high number of assaults underscore that finding.

For servicewomen who have been raped or are the victims of incest and become pregnant, the 2013 National Defense Authorization Act has repealed a ban, in effect since 1981, on the use of military insurance to pay for abortions for these types of pregnancies. New Hampshire Senator Jeanne Shaheen introduced the repeal measure because "it was blatantly unfair to women putting their lives on the line. Before the bill's passage, military women have been put in a situation that has not applied to anybody else. Even if you're in federal prison and you are raped you can get abortion coverage. That has not been true for military women since the early eighties."[19]

Since former Secretary of Defense Leo Panetta repealed the ban on women serving in combat, the VA and DoD medical systems cannot afford to be caught resting on their respective laurels when it comes to providing quality health care for veterans and active duty service women. More research still needs to be conducted regarding how combat affects women's physical and mental health. Today, most of the empirical data still focuses on men.

These women have sacrificed for their country. Now it is time for their country to sacrifice for them by keeping them healthy, long after they have finished their time in service.

NOTES

1. Anyone who wishes more information about fibromyalgia should go to the Website of the National Fibromyalgia Association at http://www.fmaware.org/.

2. U.S. Department of Veterans Affairs, Public Health, "Gulf War Veterans' Medically Unexplained Illnesses." Accessed at http://www.publichealth.va.gov/exposures/gulfwar/medically-unexplained-illness.asp.

3. Thomas Shriver, Amy Miller, and Sherry Cable, "Women's Involvement in the Gulf War Illness Movement," *Sociological Quarterly* 44.4 (Autumn 2003): 639–658.

4. U.S. Department of Veterans Affairs, Public Health, "Agent Orange." Accessed at http://www.publichealth.va.gov/exposures/agentorange/index.asp.

5. Committee on Gulf War and Health, Gulf War and Health , Vol. 5: Infectious Diseases , "Summary " (Washington: National Academies Press, 2007).

6. Research Advisory Committee on Veterans' Illnesses, "Gulf War Illnesses and the Health of Gulf War Veterans: Scientific Findings and Recommendations" (Washington: U.S. Government Printing Office, 2008), 22. Accessed at http://www.va.gov/RAC-GWVI/docs/Committee_Documents/GWIandHealthofGWVeterans_RAC-GWVIReport_2008.pdf.

7. Committee on Gulf War and Health, *Gulf War and Health* Vol. 9: *Treatment for Chronic Multisymptom Illness* (Washington: National Academy Press, 2013). Accessed at www.nap.edu.

8. Kelly Kennedy, "Study Provides More Clues to Gulf War Illness and Hope," *USA Today,* November 26, 2012.

9. Ibid.

10. Ibid.

11. "New Vets Showing Gulf War Illness Syndrome," *Army Times,* January 1, 2013. Accessed at http://www.armytimes.com.

12. National Research Council, Gulf War and Health , Vol. 4: Health Effects of Serving in the Gulf War (Washington: National Academies Press, 2006), 13.

13. Sharon Cohen, "Yahoo news," Dec 2, 2006. Accessed at http://www.news.yahoo.com/s/ap/20061203/ap_on_re_us/wounds_of_war&printer=1.

14. Kelly, *Study Provides.*

15. U.S. Army Physical Disability Agency, "Army Physical Disability Evaluation System (APDES): An Overview of the MEB/PEB Process," 16 March 2007. Accessed at http://www.pdhealth.mil/downloads/Army_Physical_Disability_Evaluation_System_%28APDES%29.pdf.

16. U.S. Department of Veterans Affairs, National Center for PTSD, "Traumatic Stress in Female Veterans," 25 February 2010. Accessed at http://www.ptsd.va.gov/professional/pages/traumatic_stress_in_female_veterans.asp.

17. Requirements for the different protective levels can be found at http://www.fas.org/nuke/guide/usa/doctrine/usaf/32401200.pdf.

18. U.S. Government Accountability Office, "DOD Health Care Domestic Health Care for Female Service Members," GAO-13-205 (29 January 2013). Accessed at http://www.gao.gov/products/GAO-13-205.

19. Allison Yarrow, "Shaheen Amendment Expands Female Service Members Access to Abortion," *Women in the World*, January 3, 2013. Accessed at http://www.thedailybeast.com/articles/2013/01/03/shaheen-amendment-expands-female-service-members-access-to-abortion.html.

Epilogue

Marching as to War—Final Thoughts

There are still a lot of unresolved racial issues in the U.S., and they spill over into every walk of life and every workplace. When I go somewhere new, people tend to look at me differently, mostly because of who I am, and it is the subtle way that people treat me differently that makes it challenging. The unfortunate fact is that being a black woman is a constant struggle.
—S. Rochelle Kimbrell, major, United States Air Force F 16 pilot

Those of us females who have been in the military for a few years have our own stories of being the first this or the first that. In some ways we each had to break through in our own way proving we were just as good as the men.
—U.S. Rep. L. Tammy Duckworth (D-Ill.)

No one ever expected me to be a part of history.
—Gidgetti Greathouse, Operation Desert Storm

A decade has passed since Army Specialist Shoshana Johnson, the first African American female POW, spent twenty two days as a captive of Iraqi insurgents. On April 13, 2003, Marines rescued her, four male members of her unit and two helicopter pilots. The painful ordeal for the former Army cook had ended. Her liberation was a strategically successful Marine rescue mission. "They showed up just like in those action movies. They broke down the door and busted inside with their weapons aimed. They had everyone get down on the floor. They asked us to stand up if we were Americans. I knew then we were going home."[1]

Again I watched Shoshana's story unfold on CNN, this time with relief. As Shoshana disembarked from the military aircraft and hobbled painfully down the flight line, she no longer looked like the frightened, vulnerable young woman that I saw in the grainy video images shown when she was first captured. Grim yet doggedly determined to move under her own power, she slowly walked past a horde of media toward freedom and a renewed life with her daughter and anxiously awaiting family members. Shoshana Johnson had become one of America's newest war heroes.

The women interviewed for this book all said they believed that the sacrifice Shoshana made for this country was above and beyond the call of duty. They expressed dismay that her story did not get the attention that Jessica Lynch received.

The interviewees did not see their own stories of service in the Gulf as special or spectacular. They expressed great pride in having served, even though some of them were initially reluctant to go to war or to see others go. "Military service is not for everyone," Jacquelyn Cofield cautioned. Even after twenty-four years of service, she had reservations about Operation Iraqi Freedom and was reticent to urge young African Americans to enlist for that conflict. Others confessed that their Gulf deployment had been anything but easy. Combating sexism and racism took its toll on several.

"As an African Jamaican American woman who served in the Persian Gulf I got to see the best and worst of people I thought were above petty nonsense. I really would do it over again, just differently," Hearther Overstreet said.

Finally, while all agreed that their time in the Gulf was personally and professionally life-changing, each woman interviewed looked on the experience as a reality of performing their military duty. "No one expected me to be a part of history," Gidgetti Greathouse stated. Just "doing our job" included abruptly leaving behind young children and spouses and friends, putting themselves in harm's way, risking their health. Doing their jobs ultimately became a crucial part of the individual and collective process undertaken to help bring victory for coalition forces. Some women said that they wondered whether they would make it through their time in the desert. They might not have lasted had they not been able to build friendships in their units, maintain their faith in God, and rely on the support of their families back home. Kim Hatcher says, "I enjoyed the military. I am more appreciative of the things I have."

Each woman interviewed strongly supported the idea that the stories of African American women also deserve to be told so that black women might find their unique place in history.

"It's a story that must be told," Felicia Weston said. "We've been underrepresented and underappreciated."

"We don't see enough of it," Gwendolyn Sheppard affirms, echoing Felicia's sentiments about the recognition due these female service members through American history.

Perhaps the narratives of these military pioneers can serve as a literary source of encouragement and empowerment for the next generation of African American servicewomen. "Telling our stories can encourage young black girls and let them know that they can do anything. They can be a part of history. They don't have to fit the negative stereotypes the media portrays," Gidgetti said.

Finally, Hearther said that their stories should be told because "we all had different experiences."

As stated earlier, the primary purpose of *Marching as to War* is to feature the lives of a group of black female officers and enlisted servicewomen from the Army, Navy, and Air Force who show facets of the professional, sociological, and interpersonal experiences of most black women during the two Gulf wars. Their narratives were candidly and poignantly shared.

Now their stories must be shared. African American feminist Anna Julia Cooper cautioned in 1892 that narratives such as these should be carefully collected, preserved, and passed on by black women to the succeeding generations. Otherwise, the historical significance of black women and their accomplishments will be overlooked or forgotten. In 1989 Charity Adams Earley, commander of the 6888th Central Postal Directory Battalion in World War II, best summarized the possible plight of African American service women's possible loss of legacy:

> The future of women in the military seems assured. . . . What may be lost in time is the story of how it happened. The barriers of sex and race were, and sometimes still are, very difficult to overcome, the second even more than the first. During World War II women in the service were often subject to ridicule and disrespect even as they performed satisfactorily. . . . Each year the number of people who shared the stress of these accomplishments lessens. In another generation young black women who join the military will have scant record of their predecessors who fought on the two fronts of discrimination—segregation and reluctant acceptance by males.[2]

Cooper's warning, coupled with Earley's, calls for continued research on African American women's contribution to the U.S. military. As part of that call, stories like these should continue to be told as African American women continue marching as to war.

NOTES

1. Diana Valdez, "Former Iraqi POW Still Haunted by Ambush," *El Paso Times*, March 25, 2013. Accessed at http://www.military.com/daily-news/2013/03/25/former-iraq-pow.

2. Quoted in Kathryn Sheldon, "Brief History of Black Women in the Military," Web site, Women in Military Service for America Memorial Foundation, Inc. Accessed at http://www.womensmemorial.org/Education/BBH1998.html#7.

Bibliography

Alexander, Rudolph. *Racism, African Americans and Social Justice.* Lanham, MD: Rowman and Littlefield, 2005.

Anderson, Kathryn, and Dana C. Jack. "Learning to Listen: Interview Techniques and Analyses." In *Women's Words: The Feminist Practice of Oral History*, edited by Sherna Gluck and Daphne Patai. New York: Routledge, 1991.

Ansen, David. "Inside the Hero Factory." *Newsweek,* 148.17 (23 October, 2006): 70–71.

Bailey, Margaret E. *The Challenge: Autobiography of Colonel Margaret E. Bailey.* Chicago: Tucker, 1999.

Bellafaire, Judith. "Volunteering for Risk: Black Military Women Overseas During the Wars in Korea and Vietnam." Website, Women in Military Service Memorial Foundation, Inc. Accessed at 199.236.85.13/Education/BWOHistory.html.

Bennett, Lerone Jr. *Before the Mayflower: A History of Black America.* New York: Penguin, 1989.

Bowne, Allison. "Long Tours Extend Heartache for Military Moms." *WeNews,* May 27, 2007: 1. Accessed at http://womensenews.org/story/military/070527/long-tours-extend-heartaches-military-moms#.UbJVl9gzXag.

Bragg, Janet Harmon, and Marjorie M. Kriz. *Soaring Above Setbacks: The Autobiography of Janet Harmon Bragg.* Smithsonian History of Aviation and Spaceflight Series. Washington: Smithsonian Institution Press, 1996.

Brown, Nikki. *Private Politics and Public Voices: Black Women's Activism from World War I to the New Deal.* Bloomington, IN: Indiana University Press, 2006.

Buckley, Gail. *American Patriots: The Story of Blacks in the Military from the Revolution to Desert Storm.* New York: Random House, 2000.

Carnegie, M. Elizabeth. *The Path We Tread: Blacks in Nursing Worldwide, 1854–1994*, 3d ed. Sudbury, MA: Jones & Bartlett, 1995.

Charlton, Thomas L.; Lois, Meyers; and Rebecca Sharpless. *Handbook of Oral History.* Lanham MD: Altamira, 2006.

Chinni, Dante. Jessica Lynch: Media Myth-Making in the Iraq War, *Project for Excellence in Journalism.* Pew Research Center, June 23, 2003. Accessed at www.journalism.org/node/223.

Clinton, Catherine. *The Black Soldier: 1492 to the Present.* Boston: Houghton Mifflin, 2000.

Committee on Gulf War and Health. Gulf War and Health, Vol. 5: Infectious Diseases, "Summary." Washington: National Academies Press, 2007.

———. *Gulf War and Health,* Vol. 9: *Treatment for Chronic Multisymptom Illness* Washington: National Academy Press, 2013. Accessed at www.nap.edu.

Doyle, M.L., and Shoshana Johnson. *I'm Still Standing: From Captive U.S. Soldier to Free Citizen—My Journey Home.* Touchstone; February 2011.

Earley Adams, Charity. *One Woman's Army: A Black Officer Remembers the WAC.* Texas A& M University Military History Series, #12, 2d ed. College Station, TX: Texas A&M University Press, 1996.

Embrey, Ellen, et al. "Task Force Report on Care for Victims of Sexual Assault." U.S. Department of Defense, April, 2004: 7. Accessed at http://www.defense.gov/news/May2004/d20040513SATFReport.pdf.

Fenner, Lorry. "Either You Need These Women or You Do Not: Informing the Debate on Military Service and Citizenship. " *Women in the Military,* 27 (1 January 2001).

Glaser, Barney, and Anselm Strauss, *The Discovery of Grounded Theory: Strategies for Qualitative Research.* Chicago: Aldine, 1967.

Global Security.Org. "Khobar Towers," accessed at http://www.globalsecurity.org/military/facility/khobar.htm.

Gulf War and Health Volume 9 Treatment for Chronic Multisymptom Illness. Committee on Gulf War and Health: Treatment for Chronic Multisymptom Illness. Institute of Medicine of the National Academies. *The National Academy Press* Washington, DC. www.nap.edu

Hall, Jane. *Fox News Watch,* April 18, 2007.

Hine, Darlene Clark, ed. *Black Women in America,* 2d ed., "Revolutionary War." New York: Oxford University Press, 2005.

Hinojosa, Ramon; Sberna Hinojosa; and Robin Hognas. Problems with Veteran-Family Communication During Operation Enduring Freedom/Operation Iraqi Freedom Military Deployment." *Military Medicine,* 177.2 (February 2012): 191–197.

Howard, John W. III, and Laura C. Prividera. "Rescuing Patriarchy or Saving 'Jessica Lynch': The Rhetorical Construction of the American Woman Solider." In *Women and Language,* 27.2 (2006): 89–101.

Hunton, Addie W., and Kathryn Johnson. *Two Colored Women with the American Expeditionary Force,* Brooklyn, NY: Brooklyn Eagle Press, 1920.

Research Advisory Committee on Veterans' Illnesses, "Gulf War Illnesses and the Health of Gulf War Veterans: Scientific Findings and Recommendations." Washington: U.S. Government Printing Office, 2008. Accessed at http://www.va.gov/RAC-GWVI/docs/Committee_Documents/GWIandHealthofGWVeterans_RAC-GWVIReport_2008.pdf.

Shannon J. Johnson, et al. "The Psychological Needs of the U.S. Military Service Members and their Families: A Preliminary Report." Report of the American Psychological Association Presidential Task Force on Military Deployment Services for Youth, Families and Service Members (Washington: American Psychological Association, 2007). Accessed at www.apa.org/about/policy/military-deployment-services.pdf.

Johnson, Shoshana, and M.L. Doyle. *I'm Still Standing: From Captive U.S. Soldier to Free Citizen—My Journey Home.* New York: Touchstone, 2011.

Jumper, Christina, et al. "National Military Family Association Report on the Cycles of Deployment Survey: An Analysis of Survey Responses from April–September, 2005," National Military Family Association (2005). Accessed at http://www.militaryfamily.org/assets/pdf/NMFACyclesofDeployment9.pdf.

Kelley, Michelle, et.al. "Navy Mothers Experiencing and not Experiencing Deployment: Reasons for Staying in or Leaving the Military." *Military Psychology,* 13.1 (2001): 55–71.

Kennedy, Kelly. "Study Provides More Clues to Gulf War Illness and Hope." *USA Today,* November 26, 2012.

King, Lisa. "In Search of Women of African Descent Who Served in the Civil War Union Navy," *The Journal of Negro History,* 83.4 (1998): 302–311.

Latty, Yvonne. *We Were There. Voices of Africans American Veterans from World War II to the War in Iraq.* New York: Harper Collins, 2004.

"Life After Iraq," National Public Radio report, air date May 28, 2007. Accessed at www.npr.org/templates/story/story.php?storyId=10495193.

Loeb, Vernon, and Dana Priest, "Midnight Raid Frees Captive" *San Francisco Chronicle,* April 2, 2003. Accessed at www.sfgate.com/news/article/Midnight-raid-frees-captive.

Lynch, Jessica. *I Am a Soldier Too: The Jessica Lynch Story.* New York: Vintage, 2004.

————. "Opening Statement before House of Representatives Committee for Oversight and Government Reform," YouTube, April 24, 2007. Accessed at http://www.youtube.com/watch?v=l0OyihqYfF4.

Manning, Loring. *Women in the Military: Where They Stand*, 5th ed. Washington: Women's Research and Education Institute, 2005.

Moffeit, Miles, and Amy Herdy. "Female GIs Report Rapes in Iraq War: 37 Seek Aid After Alleging Sex Assaults by U.S. Soldiers." *Denver Post*, 1/25/2004 (updated 5/18/2005). Accessed at http://www.denverpost.com/search/ci_0001913069.

Moore, Brenda L. "African-American women in the U.S. military," Armed Forces & Society 17 (spring 1991): 363–384.

————. *To Serve My Country, to Serve My Race. The Story of the Only African American WACS Stationed Overseas During World War II.* New York: New York University Press, 1996.

National Research Council. Gulf War and Health, Vol. 4: Health Effects of Serving in the Gulf War. Washington: National Academies Press, 2006.

"New Vets Showing Gulf War Illness Syndrome." *Army Times,* January 1, 2013. Accessed at http://www.armytimes.com.

Newman, Debra. "Black women in the Era of the American Revolution in Pennsylvania." *The Journal of Negro History*, 61.3 (July 1976): 276–289.

Obeirne, Kate. "A New Horror of War." *National Review* 55.7 (21 April 2003): 24.

Research Advisory Committee on Veterans' Illnesses. "Gulf War Illnesses and the Health of Gulf War Veterans: Scientific Findings and Recommendations." Washington: U.S. Government Printing Office, 2008. Accessed at http://www.va.gov/RAC-GWVI/docs/Committee_Documents/GWIandHealthofGWVeterans_RAC-GWVIReport_2008.pdf.

Ripple, Bryan. "DEOMI's New Commandant Personifies Diversity." Patrick Air Force Base, Brevard County, Florida, Website. Accessed 15 June, 1912 (updated 6/20/2012) at http://www.patrick.af.mil/news/story.asp?id=123306719.

Rose, Tricia, *Longing to Tell: The Sexual Lives of Black Women, in Their Own Words.* New York: Farrar, Straus and Giroux, 2003.

Schneider, Carl, and Dorothy Schneider. "American Women in World War I." *Social Education,* 58.2 (February 1994): 83–85.

Schubert, Frank. *Voices of the Buffalo Soldiers: Records, Reports and Recollections of Military Life and Service in the West.* Albuquerque: University of New Mexico Press, 2003.

Schultz, Jane. "Seldom Thanked, Never Praised and Scarcely Recognized: Gender and Racism in Civil War Hospitals." *Civil War History*, 48.3 (September 2002): 220–235.

Service Women's Action Network. "Quick Facts: Rape, Sexual Assault and Sexual Harassment in the Military," July 2012. Accessed at http://servicewomen.org/wp-content/uploads/2012/10/Final-RSASH-10.8.2012.pdf.

Sheldon, Kathryn. "Brief History of Black Women in the Military." Web site, Women in Military Service for America Memorial Foundation, 2007. Accessed at http://www.womensmemorial.org/Education/BBH1998.html.

Shriver, Thomas, Amy Miller, and Sherry Cable, "Women's Involvement in the Gulf War Illness Movement." *Sociological Quarterly* 44.4 (Autumn 2003): 639–658.

Taylor, Susie King. *Reminiscences of My Life in Camp with the 33d United States Colored Troops Late 1st S. C. Volunteers.* Boston: self published, 1902; repr. ed., New York: Markus Weiner, 1988.

U.S. Army, "Official Report on the 507th Maintenance Co.: An Nasiriyah, Iraq." Accessed at www.why-war.com/files/article07102003a.pdf.

U.S. Army Physical Disability Agency. "Army Physical Disability Evaluation System (APDES): An Overview of the MEB/PEB Process," 16 March 2007. Accessed at http://www.pdhealth.mil/downloads/Army_Physical_Disability_Evaluation_System_%28APDES%29.pdf.

U.S. Department of Defense. "Department of Defense Annual Report on Sexual Assault in the Military: Fiscal Year 2011," April 2012. Accessed at http://www.sapr.mil/media/pdf/reports/Department_of_Defense_Fiscal_Year_2011_Annual_Report_on_Sexual_Assault_in_the_Military.pdf.

————. "Department of Defense FY07 Report on Sexual Assault in the Military," 15 March 2008. Accessed at http://www.ncdsv.org/images/DoD_Annual_Report_on_Sexual_ Assault_in_ the_Military-FY2007_3-2008.pdf.

————. "Department of Defense Report on Military Services Sexual Assault for CY 2006," 15 March 2007. Accessed at http://www.sapr.mil/media/pdf/reports/2006-annual-report.pdf.

————. "Initiatives to Combat Sexual Assault in the Military," n.d. Accessed at http:// www.defense.gov/home/features/department_messages/ DoD_Initiatives_to_Combat_Sexual_Assault.pdf.

————. "Summary of Key Findings from Department of Defense Research." *Report of the Second Quadrennial Quality of Life Review.* 2009. Accessed at http:// www.militaryonesource.mil/12038/MOS/Reports/Quadrennial%20Quality%20of%20Life %20Review%202009.pdf.

————. "2011 Demographics: Report of the Military Community." 2012. Accessed at http:// www.militaryonesource.mil/12038/MOS/Reports/2011_Demographics_Report.pdf.

U.S. Department of Veterans Affairs. "Gulf War Veterans' Medically Unexplained Illnesses," n.d. Accessed at http://www.publichealth.va.gov/exposures/gulfwar/medically-unexplained-illncss.asp.

————. Public Health report: "Agent Orange." Accessed at http://www.publichealth.va.gov/ exposures/agentorange/index.asp.

U.S. Department of Veterans Affairs, National Center for PTSD. "Military Sexual Assault," 1 January 2007. Accessed at http://www.ptsd.va.gov/public/pages/military-sexual-trauma-general.asp.

————. "Traumatic Stress in Female Veterans," 25 February 2010. Accessed at http:// www.ptsd.va.gov/professional/pages/traumatic_stress_in_female_veterans.asp.

U.S. Government Accountability Office, "DOD Health Care Domestic Health Care for Female Service Members," GAO-13-205 (29 January 2013). Accessed at http://www.gao.gov/products/GAO-13-205.

VaJoe.com. "Survey of Military Spouses," survey of the U.S. Department of Defense (2008). Accessed at www.allmilitary.com/board/viewtopic.php?id=24752.

Valdez, Diana. "Former Iraqi POW Still Haunted by Ambush." *El Paso Times*, March 25, 2013. Accessed at http://www.military.com/daily-news/2013/03/25/former-iraq-pow.

Washburn, Patrick S. *The African American Newspaper: Voice of Freedom.* Medill Visions of the American Press Series. Evanston, IL: Northwestern University Press, 2006.

Waxman, Henry. Statement, U.S. House of Representatives. Hearing of the Committee for Oversight and Government Reform, April 24, 2007. Accessed at http:www.//oversight-archive.waxman.house.gov/story.asp?ID=1266.

Yarrow, Allison. "Shaheen Amendment Expands Female Service Members Access to Abortion." *Women in the World*, January 3, 2013. Accessed at http://www.thedailybeast.com/ articles/2013/01/03/shaheen-amendment-expands-female-service-members-access-to-abortion.html.

Younge, Gary. *United Kingdom Guardian,* April 2003.

Zerbisias, Antonia. *Toronto Star*, April 6, 2003. Accessed at www.commondreams.org/ views03/0406-04.htm.

Index

1st Armored Division Support Command, 45
1st Rhode Island Regiment, 22
3rd Forward Support Battalion, 2
5th Battalion, 2
9th/10th Cavalry, 26, 27
24th Evacuation Hospital, Long Binh, South Vietnam, 34
31st Air Defense Artillery, 37
33rd Regiment, 1st South Carolina Volunteers, 24
38th-41st infantry regiments, 26
49th Tactical Fighter Squadron, 34
82nd Engineering, 67
97th Bombardment Wing, 41
99th Fighter Squadron. *See* Tuskegee airmen
159th Air National Guard Civil Engineer Squadron, 84
332nd Air Expeditionary Wing. *See* Tuskegee Airmen
400th Personnel Services Company, 45
507th Maintenance Company, 2, 3, 4, 6
4404th Wing, 44, 57n2
6668th Postal Directory Battalion, 48
6888th Central Postal Directory Battalion, 31

A Voice from the South, 15
abaya, 79
abortions after sex crimes, 108

Abu Dubai, 69, 85, 86, 105
accountability, sex crime investigation, 89, 90, 91
Achilles, 9
Adams Earley, Charity, 19, 30–31
administrative punishment, 48, 89
adultery, 78, 84, 85, 89
Advanced Individual Training (AIT), 48, 52, 70
advancement military, 12, 45, 55, 80, 88, 96
advocates, sex crime victim, 90, 92
Aeronautical School of Engineering, 33
Afghanistan: conflicts, 7, 62, 99; health conditions in, 100; MST, 103; native women, 103; women combat roles in, 56
African American media, 10
African American women, 29; collective voice of, 15; first enlisted in Army, 27; first general in Air Force, 20; first helicopter pilot in Coast Guard, 37; first naval ship commander, 36; first pilot in Air Force, 36; first pilot in armed forces, 36; first pilot in Coast Guard, 37; first pilot in Marines, 36; first pilot in Navy, 36; first prisoner of war, 2, 5; first sergeant major, 35; Gulf wars story, 14; history of, 17, 111; in Gulf Wars, 12, 14; killed in military, 55; invisibility of, 15; nurses, 27, 31; telling

their stories, 15; veterans, 21
African culture, 13
agent orange herbicide, 98
Air Force, 15, 16, 19, 52, 63, 81;
    advancement opportunity in, 81;
    enlistment, 69; first African American
    female pilots in, 36; first African
    American general in, 20; integration of,
    34; nurses, 34; public affairs, 20
Air Force Academy, 34, 36, 51
Air Force Officer Candidate School, 34
Air Force Reserve, 51, 77
Air National Guard, 51, 69, 77, 106
Air Reservist Wing, 84
Airborne Warning and Control System E3
    Sentry. *See* AWACS
aircraft maintenance, 63, 64, 85
Alexander, Rudolph, 11
All American girl ideal, 11
all-volunteer military, 35
American Civil Liberties Union, 56
American Expeditionary Force, 28
American Oral History Association, 14
American Psychological Association Task
    Force, 74
American Revolution, 12, 17, 45; African
    American women in, 12; African
    Americans in, 21, 21–22
An Nasiriya, 2, 3
ANC, 28, 31, 34, 35
Anderson, Kathryn, 13
Ansen, David, 9
anti-nerve agent pills, 99
"anything goes" attitude, 85
anxiety attack, 104
Applebaum, Anne, 4
aptitude test, military, 30
Armed Forces Sexual Assault Advisory
    Council, 89
armor combat units, women in, 55
Armor, 4
Armour, Vernice, 36
arms training, 44
Army Air Corps, 33, 34
Army Nurses Corps. *See* ANC
Army Rangers, 7
Army Reserve, 55, 73
Army Times, 99

Army, 15, 16, 19, 59, 101; enlistment, 27,
    59; integration of, 34; women in
    combat in, 55, 56; mission, 20; Nursing
    Corps, 34
Arnett, Peter, 6
artillery, 1, 47, 55
Aspin, Les, 4
ass to mouth sickness. *See* ATM sickness
Associated Press poll, 62
ataxia, 99
ATM sickness, 101
authority, asserting, 83
autobiographical narratives, 12
autonomic nervous system damage, 99
aviation brigade, 52
aviators, African American woman, 36–37
avoidance strategies, 78
AWACS, 16, 63, 64
awards and decorations, race and, 83

B 52H bomber crash, 41–43
bacteria, 101
Bagdad, 51, 53, 54, 70, 72
Bailey, Margaret, 31, 32
Baldwin, Jane P., 55
Bamberg, Germany, 65
ban, women in combat, 62–63
base camp communication, 86
basic training, 52
Basra, 54
bathroom lines, 100, 101
battlefield nurses, 25
Bedouins, 63
behavior: change in, 106; problems, 75
Bennett, Lerone Jr., 23
Bentwaters, England, 41
Berington, Lucy, 25
Bethune, Mary McLeod, 29, 30
Birmingham, England, 31
birth: control during deployment, 108;
    defects, 97
Black Congressional Caucus, 10
Black Hawk helicopter, 46
"blame the victim" assault investigations,
    88
"blue suiter", 81
Blytheville, Arkansas, 42, 57n1
body armor, 67
Bohnstengel, Sandra, 97

Boston Commonwealth, 23
Bostrom, Robert, 13
Bowen, Clotilde, 34
Bradley fighting vehicle systems, 55
Bragg, Rick, 10
brain, changes in, 99
bravery, African American, 21
bravery, gender and, 1
British Army, black soldiers in, 21
British Ethiopian Regiment, 21
bronchitis, 96
Bronze Star, 34, 37
Brown Evelyn, 34
Brown University, 15
Brown, Willa, 32, 33
Buffalo Soldiers, 11, 26–27, 27
Bumiller, Elizabeth, 91
"burning semen", 97
Bush, George H.W. Administration, 4
Bush, George W., 43

Cable News Network. *See* CNN
Cable, Sherry, 98
California Air National Guard, 51
Camp Grant, Illinois, 28
Camp Patriot, 73
Camp Sherman, Ohio,, 28
cancer, 98
Cannon Air Force Base, New Mexico, 36
care of black servicemen, 28
cargo missions, 47–48, 73
Carl Schneider, 28
Carnegie, M. Elizabeth, 25, 27, 31
carriers, women on, 35
Cathay, William. *See* Williams, Cathay
Catholic University of America, 35
censorship, home communication, 71
CENTAF, 43–44
Central Command Air Forces, 57n2
Central Washington University, 4
CFS, 99
chain of command, 90
change, cultural, 13
chaplains, women, 35
Charleston, South Carolina, 22
chemical warfare gear, 48, 64, 74, 103
child custody rule, 52
childcare, 12, 16, 61, 64–65, 68, 70, 72;
    cost, 69; policy, 65

children: calls to, 68, 71; deployment and,
    73, 74; statistics on deployment, 62;
    effect on, 59–62, 112; Kuwaiti, 73;
    leaving, 16, 66; relationship with, 70,
    72; return to, 67, 68, 71; worry about,
    75
Chinni, Dante, 6
Christian Science Monitor, 6
chronic: fatigue syndrome, 96, 97; multi-
    symptom illness (CMI), 99; pain, 96, 97
church, African American, 29
CIA, 7
Circle for Negro War Relief, 29
Civil Air Patrol, 33, 36
civil engineers, 51, 84
Civil Rights Movement, 13
civil rights organizations, 28
Civil War: hospitals, 25; African
    Americans in, 21, 23–26
Civilian Pilot Training Program, 33, 34
class relationships, 13
cleanliness. *See* hygiene
Clinton, Catherine, 21
Clinton, Hillary, 23
CMI research, 99
CNN, 45, 62, 111
Coast Guard, 32, 37, 81
Cochran, Jacqueline, 33
coding. *See* processing data.69
Coffee School of Aeronautics, 33
Coffey, Cornelius, 33
Cofield, Jacquelyn, 81–82, 95, 101, 112
cognitive health, 99
Cohen, Sharon, 100
Columbia University Graduate School of
    Journalism, 5
combat, 12; African American women in,
    45–46; engineers, 55; exclusion policy,
    end of, 4; sex crimes in field, 91;
    women in, 36, 37, 45, 62, 77, 108
Combined Air Operations Centers
    (CAOC), 84
come-on lines, 78
Committee on Gulf War and Health, 99
communication, family, 68, 71
communications, 55
community service auxiliaries, 29
compensation, government medical, 95

confidentiality, sex crime victim, 89, 90, 92
conflicts with others, 46
Congress, 4, 7, 23, 26, 34, 55, 80, 89, 92, 98; 107th, 24; report to, 81
congressional hearings, 4, 91
Congressional Record, 88
Connecticut Air National Guard, 83–84
Continental Army: African Americans in, 21, 22; women in, 22
contract nurses, 25
convoy, 16, 48, 51–54, 95, 101
Coolidge, Calvin, 29
Cooper, Anna Julia, 15
Cooper, Gary, 9
Cotton Fannie Jean, 34
cough, 96, 101
counselors. *See* therapists
courier, 69
Cuba, 27
cultural: appreciation, 81; wisdom, 13
Curtis, Austin M., 27
Curtis, Namahyoke, 27

Dana, Jack, 13
data collection in sex crimes, 90, 92
Davis, Benjamin Jr., 20
Davis, Nelson, 23
death, fear of, 17
Declaration of Independence, 21
Defense Equal Opportunity Institute. *See* DEOMI
Defense Officer Manpower Personnel Management Act. *See* DOPMA
Defense Race Relations Institute, 81
Defense Sexual Assault Incident Database, 92
defense, base, 48, 63
Delta force, 56
Denver Post, 88, 91
DEOMI, 81
Department of Defense, 106
Department of Defense 2011 Demographics Report . . ., 62
Department of Defense. *See* DoD and by subject
Department of Veterans Affairs, 88, 98, 107

dependency discharge. *See* hardship discharge
Dependent Pension Act of 1890, 23
deployment: and family report, 68; as escape, 70; rotation, 71; stress, 75, 97; with health problems, 104
depression, 97, 99
Deputy Commander of Maintenance, 63
desegregation of armed forces, 34
desert beauty queen, 77, 78, 85
Dhahran, Saudi Arabia, 43, 44, 48, 50, 78, 79, 87, 92n1, 96, 104
diarrhea, 101
Dick, Kirby, 91
Diego Garcia Navy Base, 41, 42
diet, 96
dining area, 101
discrimination against African American women, 29, 34, 55, 105
disparity in media coverage, 12
diversity, 81
divorce, 75
documentary on rape in military, 91
DoD: survey, 75; sex crime policies, 91–92; women in combat lawsuit, 55, 56; health programs, 107–109
DOPMA, 35
Drill Sergeant School, 37
drinking water, 100
Dubois, W.E.B., 29
Duckworth, L. Tammy, 111

Eaker Air Force Base, 41, 42, 57n1, 96
eating disorders, 107
emergency leave, 65
emotional, 106; healing therapy, 105; health, 95; pain, 106
engineers, women, 35
enlistment, reasons for, 45
equal opportunity, 80, 81
Escon Village, Saudi Arabia, 63
ethnic hair products, 102
Europe deployment, 41
Executive Branch, 4
Executive Order 9981, 34
exercise, 96
eye wounds, 105

F-16 fighter, 36, 82

F-16 Fighter Wing, 81
family, 68; as unit, 82; care of, 29, 72;
    deployment and, 59, 64, 112; sacrifice
    of, 59; separation, 17, 60; support, 71,
    112; unity, 68
Family Care Plan, 72
Family Day picnics, 20
Father's Day, 73
fatigue, 96, 97, 99
fear in combat areas, 103
female health issues, 108
female slaves on plantations, 22
feminist movement. *See* Women's
    Movement.67
Fenner,, Lorry M., 1, 37
fibromyalgia, 97, 109n3
fidelity, marital, 85
field: artillery radar, 55; hospitals in
    Korean war, 34
first responders in sex crimes, 108
Fleet Logistics Squadron Forty, 36
Florence, Arizona, 31
FMS, 99
focus groups, 89
follow up medical appointments, 107
"force protection" guidelines, 90
forensic evidence of sex crimes, 90
Fort Bliss, Texas, 2
Fort Des Moines, 30
Fort Dix, New Jersey, 47
Fort Gordon, Georgia, 48
Fort Hill Cemetery, 23
Fort Jackson, South Carolina, 48
Fort Lawton, Washington, 60
Fort Leonard, Maryland, 68
Fort Monroe, Virginia, 23
Fort Riley, Kansas., 65
fortifications, slaves' work on, 22
Fox News Watch, 8
frat boy mentality, 78
fraternization, 77
Freedman's Hospital, 27
freedom, African American struggle for,
    21
"friendly fire", 7

Gallup polls, 62
GAO, 108
gas masks. *See* chemical warfare gear

gastrointestinal disorders, 97, 99
Gates, Robert M., 59
genealogy, 13
Georgia, 71
GI Jane persona, 6
Glaser, Barney, 14
Gloudon, Barbara, 1
Government Accountability Office (GAO),
    108
government medical compensation, 95
Great Britain, 79
Greathouse, Gidgetti, 47–48, 87, 100, 101,
    102, 103, 106, 111, 112
Greeks, 13
Grenada, invasion of, 45
grief, 45–43
griots. *See* storytellers.65
grounded theory, 14
group therapy, 105
guard duty, 67
Guidelines for oral history, 14
Gulf War illness. *See* Gulf War syndrome
Gulf War syndrome, 17, 97–99, 105, 107
Gulf Wars. *See* Operation Desert Shield;
    Operation Desert Storm; Operation
    Iraqi Freedom

hair: damage, 95, 102; products, 102;
    styles, 102
Haley, Robert, 99
Haley, 99
Hall, Jane, 8
Hampton (Virginia) University, 45, 46
hardship discharge, 59, 65, 66
Haring, Ellen L., 55
Harman, Jane, 90
Harmon Bragg, Janet, 32, 33, 34
Harris, Marcelite, 34
Hatcher, Kim, 59, 100
Hayes, Marcella A., 36
hazardous chemicals, 105
HC 130 airplane, 37
headaches, 97, 105
health, 17; battlefield, 98; care, 12, 16,
    108; emotional, 95; mental, 95; of
    women, 100, 108; physical, 95;
    problems, 73, 104, 105, 112; sacrifices,
    95, 96
heart problems, 101

heat, extreme, 96, 100, 101, 103
heavy metals, 101
Hegar vs. Panetta, 56
helicopter pilots, 35
Hemmons-Carter, Mildred, 34
Henderson, Alice, 35
Herdy, Amy, 88
hernia, 105
"Highway of Death", 16, 47
Hine, Darlene Clark, 22
Hinjosa, Ramon, 71
Hinojosa, Sberna, 71
Hogansville, Georgia, 59
Hognas, Robin, 71
holistic health remedies, 96
Hollin, Evelyn, 37
Holmes, La'Shanda, 37
Hooker, Olivia J., 32
Hooks, Bell, 15
Hoover, Herbert, 29
Hopper, Christina, 36
hospitals, Civil War, 25
House of Representatives Committee on
    Oversight and Government Reform, 7
housing facilities, 28, 82, 92n1
Howard, John, 8
Howard, Michelle, 36
human relations, 81
Hunter Auxiliary Airfield, Savannah,
    Georgia, 52
Hunton, Addie, 28
Hussein, Qusay, 51–52
Hussein, Saddam, 43, 51
Hussein, Uday, 51–52
hygiene, 100–101

"I Am a Soldier Too", 10
I'm Still Standing, 10
IEDs, 74
Iliad, 9
illness, Gulf War. *See* by type of illness
Image, 4
immunity to fever, assumption of, 27
improvised explosive devices. *See* IEDs
Indian Ocean, 42
indifferent care of black troops, 28
Infantry, 4, 36, 55, 87
insect repellent, 99
Institute of Medicine, 99, 100

International Coalition Forces, 82
international military protocol, 80
International Oral History Association, 14
Internet café, 73
interracial couples in South, 69
interviews, 12, 16, 44; inductive, 14;
    standards for, 14
intimate relationships of veterans, 104
investigation of sex crimes, 89, 92
invisibility of African American women,
    15
Iraq conflict, 16, 62, 89, 106; PTSD and,
    103; deployment, 72, 84; MST, 103; no
    fly zone, 36, 43, 44; African American
    women in, 51–54, 55; health conditions
    in, 100, 101; women, 103; women's
    military roles in, 55
Iraqi: fighter planes, 44; forces, 2
irritable bowel syndrome, 99
Islamic law on social contact, 103
Italy, 81

Japan, 34
Jeter, Phoebe, 35
Jim Crow military policies, 29
Johnson, Hazel, 35
Johnson, James Weldon, 29
Johnson, Kathryn, 28
Johnson, Lyndon, 34
Johnson, media treatment of, 2, 5, 11
Johnson, Patricia, 48–49, 68, 85, 86, 101,
    103, 105, 106
Johnson, Shoshana, 10, 41, 77; captivity
    of, 1, 2; capture of, 2, 16, 17, 54, 74;
    investigative report, 2; media reporting
    regarding, 4, 5, 9, 12; rescue of, 111
Jordan, 83, 84
judge advocate, 52

Kelly, Mildred C., 35
Kensington Press, 10
Khobar Towers, 79, 82, 92n1, 96
Kim Hatcher, 65–67, 112
Kimbrell, S. Rochelle, 111
Kimbrell, Shawna, 36
King Taylor, Susan, 24–25, 25
King, Edward, 25
King, Lisa, 25
King, Teresa, 37

Korat, Thai Air Base, Thailand, 34
Korean War, 19; veterans of, 20; African
  American women in, 34
Kuwait. *See* by subject

Lackland Air Force Base, San Antonio,
  Texas, 81
Laird, Melvin, 80, 81
land mines, 47
Landstuhl Regional Medical Hospital, 7
Larson, Mary, 13
latrines, 95, 103; cleanliness of, 101;
  condition of, 100, 101; location of, 101
laundering uniforms, 100
lawsuit against Army and Department of
  Defense, 55
life threads, 15
Lindsay, Diane, 34
Little Creek Amphibious Base, Virginia
  Beach, 73
Little, Harriet, 25
Little, Samuel, 25
Loeb, Vernon, 7
Lori, 10
lung problem, 106
Lynch committee testimony, 8
Lynch, Jessica, 4, 5, 10, 112; as ideal, 11;
  capture of, 3, 10; injuries, 7; media
  treatment of, 5, 7; myth, 6–7; rescue of,
  5, 6

M1 Abrams tank, 55
Magazine, 6
malaria, 27
male: culture, 77, 84, 86; escort in Islamic
  setting, 87; superiors, 85
malingering, charge of, 95, 96, 105
Malveaux, Julianne, 1
Marines, 9, 15, 111; integration of, 32;
  nurses in, 32; African American female
  pilot in, 36; resistance to African
  American women, 34; women in, 55,
  56
marriage, 78; deployments and, 16;
  dysfunctional, 69; fidelity, 85; military
  tradition, 3
MASH units, 34, 50
Martin, Edwina, 34
massacre, 41

McIntosh Menze, Jeanne, 37
media, 4, 8, 10, 44; dealing with, 42;
  female POWs in, 5, 7; queries, 44; race
  and, 12; reporting, 11; spin, 8
medical: discharge, 106; evaluation, 101;
  history, 97
medication during deployment, 108
medics, 55
memory loss, 97, 99, 107
Memphis, Tennessee, 42
menopause, 107
mental health, 95, 107, 108; families needs
  for, 61, 74, 75; pain, 106; sex crime
  victim needs for, 108
meritocracy, 80, 93n2
methodology, 13–15; plus more, 16
Miles Foundation, 89
military: academies, women in, 35;
  benefits, 89; doctors, 96, 104; family
  grief, 42; family life, 19, 20, 59–62, 66,
  67, 74, 75; family research, 74, 75;
  family tradition, 45; history, 1, 5, 19,
  20; insurance for abortions, 108; justice
  system, 89; misinformation, 7, 8;
  police, women in, 35, 48, 55;
  regulations, 102; segregation in, 28;
  tradition, 19, 20
Military Health System, 107, 108
military sexual trauma. *See* MST
Miller, Amy, 98
minefield, 48
missile attacks, 35, 47, 48, 49–50, 51, 74,
  82, 100, 103, 104
Mission Oriented Protective Posture 4. *See*
  MOPP 4
"mixed multitude.", 22
Mobile Army Surgical Hospitals. *See*
  MASH units
Moffeit, Miles, 88
Monrovia, Liberia, 31
Montgomery, James, 23
Moore, Brenda, 27
Mopp 4, 103
morale, 91; call, 68, 72; black troop, 29
Morgan, Carolyn, 69–70, 77, 85–86, 95,
  102, 105–106, 106
Mother's Day, 59, 73
mothers in combat, 62–63, 75
movie, 6

MSNBC, 6
MST, 88, 103, 106
multiple chemical sensitivity, 97
multiple launch rocket system, 55
multiracial environment, 81
multi-symptom illnesses, 97
Murray, John [Lord Dunmore], 21
mutaween, 43
mutual support, veteran, 106
mystery illnesses, 95, 97

NAAA, 33
narrative history. *See* oral history/narrative
    chronicle
National Airmen's Association of
    America. *See* NAAA
National Association of Black Military
    Women, 21
National Association of Colored Women,
    29
National Center for PTSD, 106
National Council of Negro Women, 29
National Defense Authorization Act, 108
National Fibromyalgia Association, 109n3
National Guard, women in, 15, 35
National Military Family Association, 68
National Public Radio, 11
National Sex Offenders Registry, 89
Native American: prejudice toward
    Piestewa as, 10; first woman combat
    fatality, 3; first woman POW, 10
NATO military exercises, 63
Naval Medical Corps, 35
naval reservist, 104
Naval Station Great Lakes Hospital, 107
Navy, 15, 25, 73, 104; African American
    female, 35; nurses, World War II, 32;
    desegregation of, 32, 34; African
    American female pilot in, 36; African
    American woman ship commander in,
    36; Union, 25
Navy Reserve, 51
Navy SEALS, 36, 56
NBC, 6, 10
negative coverage, Iraq fighting, 6
"Negro race" empowerment, 29
neurotoxins, 99
New Bern Navy Hospital, 25
New York Times, 91

New Zealand Herald, 11
news reports and PTSD, 105
newspapers, 6, 44
Newsweek, 9
Nietzsche, Friedrich, 88, 93n7
Nightingale, Florence, 98
Nike-Hercules missile system, 20
Nixon, Sergeant, 47
no fly zone, 36, 43, 44
noncombat jobs, 41
Noriega, Manuel, 45
North Carolina State University, Durham,
    51
North Dakota State University, 72
North Vietnamese, 105
number deployed servicewomen, 62
nurses, 23; African American, 22, 25, 31;
    contract, 25

oath, enlistment, 59
officer evaluation reports, 46
officers, African American women, 77
oil field fires, Kuwait, 64, 96, 105
oil well fire smoke, 96
Okinawa, 34
One Woman's Army, 30
One Wrong Turn, 10
Operation Desert Shield: African
    American Women in, 43, 65; story of,
    43. *See also* by subject
Operation Desert Storm: African American
    women in, 35, 43–44, 55, 63, 65; family
    study in, 61; PTSD, 103; story of, 43,
    82; women in combat in, 55. *See also*
    by subject
Operation Enduring Freedom, 37
Operation Iraqi Freedom. *See* by subject
Operation Just Cause, 45, 48, 68
Operation Northern Watch, 36
Operation Urgent Fury, 45
oral histories/narratives, 12, 13, 17
orientation briefing, 87
Orr, Deborah, 11
orthopedic conditions, 97, 101
"overage" troop reduction, 106
Overstreet, Hearther, 85, 101, 112

pain, 96, 97, 99, 105
Panama, invasion of, 10, 45, 48, 68

Panetta, Leon, 56, 91, 108
paralyzed larynx, 101
Paris, 31
Patrick AFB, Florida, 52, 81
Patriot missiles, 2, 35, 50, 64, 103
pay, military, 80
Pentagon, 5, 7, 8
Persian Gulf War sexual survey, 88
Persian War Gulf Veterans Act, 98
Personnel and Manpower Division, 84
Philippines, 34
physical: health, 95, 108; needs of sex
    crime victims, 108
Pickens, Harriet, 32
Piestewa, Lori Ann, 3, 4; media treatment
    of, 5; memorial service for, 11
pilot's license, 33
"piss ditch", 101
Pittsburgh Courier, 32
pleurisy, 96
poetry, 13
policies, sexual assault report, 90
Post Deployment Health Assessment, 107
postal clerk specialist, 48, 68
post-deployment medical checkup, 96
post-traumatic stress disorder. *See* PTSD
Pound, Ezra, 19
Powell, Colin, 80
powerlessness of low rank, 87
POWs, 74, 77; first, 9, 10, 17; injuries,
    111; media focus on, 2; pilot, 82;
    women, 4, 5
prednisone, 106
pregnancy, 17, 108
prejudice in military. *See* racism
preserving history, 13
press, African American, 28, 29, 32
pressure, sexual, 85
Priest, Dana, 7
Prividera, Laura, 8
processing data, 14
profile three (P-3) duty restriction, 101
The Project for Excellence in Journalism, 5
promotions. *See* advancement., 12, 35, 83,
    96
prosecution in sex crime cases, 89, 91, 92
protection for sexual assault victim, 90
psychiatric illnesses, 97, 98
"The Psychological Needs . . .", 74

psychological stress, 98
psychosomatic illness, 95
PTSD, 17, 97, 103–104, 106; counseling,
    104–106; research, 106
public: affairs, 5, 42, 43, 44, 96; relations,
    wartime, 9
pulmonary disorders, 101
punishment for sexual crimes, 88, 89

Qatar, 81, 82, 84, 86
Quillan, Maria, 41, 59, 73, 103–104, 106

race: equality, struggle for, 80; in military,
    81; relations in U.S., 80, 81, 111;
    prejudice, 69
racism, 16; toward servicewomen, 12, 83,
    87; assumptions of, 27; during Persian
    Gulf wars, 17, 80, 83; in American
    society, 21; in military, 112; toward
    African American nurses, 28, 31;
    toward African American WACs, 30;
    toward African American women
    pilots, 33–34; triumphing over, 21;
    West Point, 20
rape. *See* sexual assault
rash, skin, 97
recommendations, sexual assault policy,
    89–90
recreation and relaxation facilities, 85
Red Cross, 28
redeployment screenings, 108
reeducation, racial, 81
Reingold, Nathan, 14
Reliability of oral history, 14
religious faith, 12, 78, 84, 87, 112
Reminiscences of My Life . . ., 25
report disposition in sex crimes, 90
"Report on Sexual Assault in the Military",
    93n13
reporting sexual assaults, 88, 89, 90
rescue: POW, 6, 111; slave, 23
Research Advisory Committee on Gulf
    War Veterans' Illnesses, 98
research: framework, 14; Gulf War
    syndrome, 97; PTSD, 103; veteran
    health, 98, 108
reservists, 107
respiratory conditions, 96, 97
rest and recreation station, 69

restaurants, 87
return from deployment, 59–62, 67, 68
Reyes, Coreen, 45–46, 84, 87
rheumatologist, 97
risk, sexual assault, 90
"risk rule", 4
Riyadh, Saudi Arabia, 43, 45, 48, 50, 63, 67, 79
Roanoke, Virginia, 104
Robbins Illinois, 33
Robinson, Brenda, 36
Robinson, John, 33
rocket: grenade (RPG), 51; launchers, 47
Rodgers, Marie, 34
Roosevelt, Eleanor, 29, 33
Roosevelt, Franklin, 29
Roosevelt, Theodore, 11, 27
Roper polls, 62
Rose, Tricia, 15
ROTC, 4, 35, 45, 46
Rough Riders, 11
rules of engagement, 44, 74
rumors, wartime, 44
Rumsfeld, Donald, 6, 89
Ruth, Alfred, 25
Ruth, Harriet, 25

S.S. Tubman, 23
safety concerns, 79, 85–86
Salter, Courtney, 41, 52–54, 70–72, 84, 95, 101, 102
saluting women officers, 80
San Juan Hill, 11, 27
sand, blowing, 53, 67, 100, 102
Sanitation, 100
Santarelli, Eugene D., 43, 57n2
sarcoidosis lung infection, 105
sarin, 99
Saudi Arabia, 43, 48, 50, 64, 86, 87, 96, 97; deployment to, 68; prejudice, 79; sexual views, 43, 79–80, 86–87
Savannah, Georgia, 22
Saving Jessica Lynch, 10
Schneider, Dorothy, 28
Schubert, Frank N., 26
Schultz, Jane, 25
Schwarzkopf, H. Norman, 82
Scott, Emmett J., 28
screening interviewees, 16

SCUD missile attacks. *See* missile attacks
Sea Hawk helicopter, 37
Sea Island South Carolina, 23
Seabees, 51
security police, 86
segregation, World War II nurse, 28, 31–32
sensationalism in journalism, 7
separation anxiety, 59–62, 62, 66, 67, 68, 70, 74, 74–75
September 11 attacks, 36, 52, 104
sergeant major, first African American woman, 35
Sergeant York, 9
service illness disability, 104
Service Women's Action Network. *See* SWAN
Seward, William H., 23
sexism, 12, 16, 17, 79, 84, 85, 86, 87; during deployment, 80; military, 112; toward nurses, 31; toward WACs, 30; toward women pilots, 34
sexual: availability, assumption of, 85, 87; complaint task force, 89; expectations during deployment, 78; harassment, 12, 16, 77, 84, 87, 88, 89, 91; misconduct, defining, 89; overtures, 78; propositions, 85; trauma, 88, 107; violence survey, 108
sexual assault, 7, 84, 85, 86, 87, 88, 89, 91; counseling services, 89; data collection, 90, 92; defining, 89; Hotline, 89; information, 89; policy, 89, 90, 91, 92; prevention, 89, 90, 90–91, 91, 108; reports, 88, 89, 90; statistics, 90, 91, 108; stories, 91; studies, 91; victim advocacy, 90, 92; victim protection, 90; victims, 108
Shaheen, Jeanne, 108
Sharpless, Rebecca, 13
Shaw Air Force Base, South Carolina, 69
Sheppard, Gwendolyn, 51–52, 72, 77, 84, 101, 102, 107
Shinseki, Eric K., 107
ships, women aboard, 4
showers, 100, 101, 103
Shriver, Thomas, 98
sickness in camp, 101
sickness, spread of, 101

Signal Battalion, 48, 50
silence about sexual assault, 88
"silencing", 20
singing, 13
single moms in military, 75
sinusitis, 96
skin conditions, 97, 101
slaves, escaping, 23
sleep: patterns, 96; seizures, 101
smallpox, 25
smoke in air, 96
Soaring Above Setbacks, 32
social: conflict of 1960s, 105; historians, 13
Sociological Quarterly, 98
Soldier's Medal for Heroism, 34
sore throat, 101
South Carolina, 22
South, 21, 22
Southern Watch, 36
Southwest Asia Theater, 14
Soviets, 86
Spanish-American War, 27
Special Forces, 5, 7, 36, 51, 55
"special victims unit", 92
spoils of war, women as, 88
St. Louis, Missouri, 26
St. Simons Island, 24
stereotypes of black women, 17, 113
Stokes, Ann, 25
storytelling, 15
Stowe, Harriet Beecher, 22
Straus, Anselm, 14
stress, 96; return, 104; deployment/combat, 97, 98, 102
subject-oriented oral history style, 14
"silencing", 20
"subtle racism", 11
Sundance Film Festival, 91
Super Cobra attack helicopter, 36
support network while deployed, 87
survivor's guilt, 51
SWAN, 91
Sweetwater, Texas, 33

taped interviews, 13
targets, women as Iraqi, 74
TDY, 63, 64, 78
Television, 6, 42. *See also* by organization

temporary duty assignments. *See* TDY
Tengesdal, Merryl, 37
Tent City, Saudi Arabia, 45
Thanksgiving, 61
The Guardian, 11, 31
The Invisible War, 91
therapists, women, 107
therapy, 105. *See also* group therapy
Thomas, Cal, 8
throat symptoms, 96
Tillman, Pat, 7, 8
Tinker Air Force Base, Oklahoma, 63
Torrejon Air Base, Spain,, 81, 82
tracking sex crimes, 92
traditions, 13
training, 52, 63, 70, 92
transfer for sexual assault victims, 92
transparency in sexual assault cases, 89
transport pilots, 35
transportation, 73
trash, burning, 101
trauma specialists, 106
Treaty of Paris, 22
Trinidad, Colorado, 27
troop morale, 31
Thompson, Gladys O., 31
truck breakdowns, 47, 48
Truman, Harry S., 33, 34
trust, in women's competence, 85
Tuba City, Arizona., 10
Tubman, Harriet, 23–24
Tuchman, Barbara, 14
Tuskegee Airmen, 20, 32, 33, 36
Tuskegee Institute, 33, 34
Two Colored Women with the Expeditionary Force, 28
typhoid fever, 27

U-2 reconnaissance plane, 37
Underground Railroad, 23
Uniform Code of Military Justice, 89
Union Army, 23
Unit Control Center, 82
United Arabic Emirates, 85
University of Texas Southwestern Medical Center, 99
U.S. Army Criminal Investigative Lab, 90
U.S. Central Command Air Forces. *See* CENTAF

U.S. Central Command. *See* USCENTCOM
U.S. Colored Infantry, 23
U.S. District Court, 56
U.S., social/cultural change in, 13
U.S.S. Black Hawk, 25
U.S.S. Hartford, 25
U.S.S. Rover, 25
U.S.S. Rushmore, 36
USA Today, 62
USCENTCOM, 44

VA, 106; centers, 107; clinics, 107; compensation, 106; doctors, 105, 107; health programs, 107–109; hospitals, 51, 105, 107; medical care, 104, 108
Veterans Affairs Department. *See* VA
Veterans Enhancement Act, 98
veterans: African American, 20; narratives, 20; Gulf Wars, 98; Vietnam War, 20, 105. *See also* VA
victim, sexual assault: advocacy for, 91; care after sex crimes, 90; misconduct, 90
Vietnam War, 98; African American veterans of, 20; agent orange illness, 98; veterans, 20, 105; POWs, 5; protest, 14; African American women in, 34; deployment, 62; sexual assaults in, 88
vitamin supplements, 96
vomiting, 101

WAAC, 31; officer training, 30. *See also* WACS
WACS, 30, 31, 35
WAFS, 35
Walter Reed Army Hospital, 7
War Department, World War I, 28
war heroes, 111
warrior tradition, African American, 21
wartime heroes, 8
Washburn, Patrick, 29
washing facilities, 100
Washington Post, 4, 7
Washington, George, 21, 22
WASP, 33, 34
waste: burning, 105; removal, 101

Water Survival Training, 37
water, local, 102
WAVES, 35
West Point honor code, 20
Western frontier, 26
Weston, Felecia, 104–105
Weston, Felicia, 49–51
white America, 11
white blood count, 105
wild dogs, 86
Williams, Cathay, 26–27
Willis, Frances, 32
Women in Military Service for America Memorial Foundation, 21
women in military, 111; in combat, 3, 4, 77, 108; in Continental Army, 22; in military tradition, 4; in Saudi Arabia, 43, 79–80, 86; in World War II, 29; veterans with PTSD, 103; resentment toward, 64
Women's Armed Services Integration Act, 34
Women's Army Auxiliary Corps. *See* WAAC
Women's Army Corps. *See* WACS.
Women's Auxiliary Service Pilots. *See* WASP
Women's rights Movement, 13
Women's Services Integration Act, 35
World War I, 9; African American veterans, 20; African American women in, 26, 28–29
World War II, 19, 48; African Americans in, 20; African American Women in, 29–34; nurses, 31; women advances during, 19

yellow fever, 27
YMCA, 28
York, Alvin, 9
Yorktown, English surrender at, 22
Young Men's Christian Association. *See* YMCA
Younge, Gary, 11

Ziering, Amy, 91